WILLPOWER
IS NOT ENOUGH

WILLPOWER
IS NOT ENOUGH

Why we don't succeed at change

A. DEAN BYRD AND
MARK D. CHAMBERLAIN

DESERET BOOK COMPANY
SALT LAKE CITY, UTAH

Library of Congress Cataloging-in-Publication Data

Byrd, A. Dean, 1948–
  Willpower is not enough : why we don't succeed at change / A. Dean Byrd and Mark D. Chamberlain.
    p.   cm.
  Includes bibliographical references and index.
  ISBN 0-87579-871-3
    1. Spiritual life—Mormon Church. 2. Change—Religious aspects—Christianity. 3. Success—Religious aspects—Christianity. 4. Self-control—Religious aspects—Christianity. 5. Emotions—Religious aspects—Christianity. I. Chamberlain, Mark D., 1964–
  BX8656.B88   1995
  248.8—dc20   94-23989
                                                              CIP

Printed in the United States of America

10 9   8   7   6   5   4   3   2   1

▪ CONTENTS ▪

■ ACKNOWLEDGMENTS ■

This book came about because of "promptings of the heart." We've come to understand that helping people to change is a healing process. As professionals we perhaps are facilitators of the healing process; as people, we are recipients of that healing.

For us, the facilitators have been our wives, Jenny and Elaine, and our children, Ryan and Aaron, and Chris, David, Nicole, Ryan, and Kristen. They have all taught us that whisperings of the Spirit can be an important source of truth. It's fantastic to live with a family that believes you can do anything.

To our parents, we express appreciation for two gifts: the courage to think and the heart to follow our convictions.

Finally, we are grateful to our clients. We cherish how much they have taught us about the Savior's love.

A LEASH OR A HARNESS?

*It is contrary to the order of heaven for any soul to be locked into
compulsive immoral behavior with no way out.*

—ELDER BOYD K. PACKER

We've all known the struggle of trying to overcome habits, attitudes, and behaviors that keep us from the rich and joyful life God wants us to have. These difficulties seem to be an unavoidable part of our existence.

The frustrating thing is that we're often so ineffective in coming to the changes we want! We grit our teeth and seek to fight our inner weaknesses through sheer willpower—and then we're disappointed and discouraged when change doesn't come, or when it comes too slowly.

We've seen this problem over and over as professional counselors: people who want to gain more control over their lives but just don't seem to be able to. We've grappled with the same problem in our personal lives. As we've worked and counseled and struggled over the years, we've come to a surprising conclusion: Efforts at using willpower don't work because using willpower isn't the right way to go about changing ourselves!

We realize that this idea runs counter to the thinking and understanding of our culture at large. We in the Western culture just "know" that the way to bring changes into our lives is to exercise strict and undeviating willpower. If we fail in our efforts at change or self-control, we never think to look at our approach—instead we conclude we must have a lack of determination or a flaw in character. As a result, we figure we'll just have to try harder.

The Western culture doesn't have a monopoly on truth, however, and we've come to believe that there is a better way. The way of will-power emphasizes the power of the *mind*—just make up your mind and you can do anything.

In contrast to this is an approach that relies on the power of the *heart*. This view, which is more familiar to those of the Asian cultures, seems to run counter to many of our own cultural patterns. Yet we believe it is more consistent with the gospel of Jesus Christ.

These two views of self-control rely on differing perspectives on the nature of the self. Self-control that relies on the mind (or on will-power) is built on the assumption that the self, at the core, is evil and undesirable. It needs to be controlled and inhibited. Spontaneous feelings and actions ought to be squelched; only the rational and planned should be followed. Metaphorically, a leash and a muzzle are consistent with this view.

On the other hand, self-control that relies on the power of the heart is grounded in the assumption that the core self is good rather than inherently evil or destructive. It assumes that the self is primarily in need of nourishment, encouragement, development, cultivation, and fulfillment. This view of the self holds that it must be tamed, not with a whip, leash, or muzzle, but with a bridle or harness.

You may not be familiar with the idea of "heart power," as opposed to willpower. It may seem to contradict your current way of thinking. But as you consider the ideas carefully, you may be surprised at how consistent they are with gospel principles. And as you follow the suggestions we give in the pages that follow, you may be surprised at how much they help.

PART ONE

IF NOT WILLPOWER, THEN WHAT?

CHAPTER 1

IT TAKES MORE THAN WILLPOWER

*Jesus saith . . . I am the way, the truth, and the life: no man cometh unto
the Father, but by me.*

—JOHN 14:6

"You Can Do Anything You Put Your Mind To"?

We've had this idea drilled into us from our youngest years: You
can do anything you put your mind to. If you fail, try, try again.

Ella Wheeler Wilcox expressed the idea eloquently:

> *There is no chance, no destiny, no fate,*
> *Can circumvent or hinder or control*
> *The firm resolve of a determined soul.*[1]

Willpower is supreme. That seems to be a prevailing view in our
culture. Before they even get to preschool, our children are indoctri-
nated with this mind-set. Think about the favorite bedtime story, "The
Little Engine That Could." Its moral: If you just try hard enough, long
enough, you can do anything.

Over time the message is reinforced. Mind over matter, we learn.
Where there's a will, there's a way. You just have to want it bad enough.
And so it goes into adulthood, until we find ourselves singing the praises
of the power of the mind. What comfort it brings, the conviction that we
are the captains of our souls!

Out of the night that covers me,
Black as the Pit from pole to pole,
I thank whatever gods may be
For my unconquerable soul. . . .

It matters not how strait the gate,
How charged with punishments the scroll,
I am the master of my fate;
I am the captain of my soul.[2]

But if we are the captains of our souls, what happens when our rudder seems disconnected and powerless? What happens when the little engine can't? When our will fails us? When there's a lapse in our resolve? Our Western heritage of white-knuckled control tells us just to keep working at it—it took the little engine more than one try, didn't it?

But the fact is, sometimes our own willpower and resolve are not enough. We lose our motivation and lose control. Then "you can do anything if you put your mind to it" becomes "you *could* have done anything *if only you had* put your mind to it." That line of thinking often leads to feelings of inadequacy and guilt.

Consider the example of Ben. He and his wife had talked often about his anger. He knew it was harming his family, and he was disgusted with himself after his outbursts. He tried to control his temper, but he always seemed to have a short fuse. In his first therapy session he talked about one of the frustrating failures he'd experienced the previous week:

"Before going to sleep one night, my wife and I planned a special family night with the kids—we scheduled it for the very next night. The next day I kept thinking about how I was not going to get mad at them when I got home. I just wouldn't do it! After work I was even whistling as I walked to the car. But when I reached my car I saw a new dent on the door. Then, listening to the radio on the way home, I heard that my baseball team lost an important game. The usual traffic seemed extra slow, and when I did get home the evening was not organized the way my wife had agreed. I blew my top. I ruined the rest of the evening for the kids, and I went to bed angry with my wife."

Later in the session we set some goals for the therapy. Ben knew exactly what he wanted. "I hope you can help me develop a greater ability to resist temptation. I give in too easily. Yeah, I definitely need to become better at resisting."

Resisting: A Strategy of the Mind

Resisting. Gritting our teeth, clenching our fists, and doing what we think we should even when we don't feel like it. Forcing it. *Willpower!* That's the way we approach most of our efforts at change.

The widespread acceptance of the principles of behavioral psychology has perpetuated this approach. Behavioral psychology typically attempts to manipulate a person's external conditions in ways that will "extinguish" unwanted behaviors.

For example, some behavioral psychologists have paired undesirable fantasies with electric shock in order to make them more "aversive." Medication that causes nausea when it interacts with alcohol in the body can be used as a tool in treating problem drinking. Clients are instructed to interrupt addictive thought patterns through "thought stopping" techniques such as sharply snapping a rubber band on their wrists when their minds enter forbidden territory.

The High Cost of Resisting

The first and most obvious problem with depending exclusively on willpower to resist temptation is that, all too often, it simply fails us.

The second drawback of a continued, exclusive reliance on willpower is that it may actually serve to worsen the cycle of temptation, where we constantly vacillate between self-denial and self-indulgence. The cycle goes something like this: We make a firm resolve to control ourselves in some way. Then we're tempted, and despite our best efforts, we give in to our cravings. Following our failure, we feel guilty and vow to never falter again. Once again we're tempted, we give in, and then again resolve to be strong. And so the cycle continues.

Ironically, our constantly renewed resolution can actually fuel the forbidden desire. One example is the bulimic who, in the guilt following a binge, promises to never indulge again and to adhere to even stricter diet restrictions. Of course, this kind of resistance only increases the focus on hunger, and the roller coaster goes on—the guilt associated with the "lows" deepens, and more effort is required to reach the "highs" of resistance.

Hunger, of course, is a physiological response. But there is evidence to show that emotional or mental self-denial has a similarly self-perpetuating effect. As we seek to resist temptation, we hope that suppressing the thought will make our undesirable urges go away. But research has shown that trying to force something out of our minds actually cements it more firmly in them. In ten years of studying thought suppression, psychologist Daniel Wegner at the University of Virginia in Charlottesville discovered that attempted thought suppression brings an increase of negative emotions and physiological stress. For instance, subjects who tried not to think about sexual activity had the same level of physiological response (as measured by skin conductance level) as those who were instructed to think about sex.[3]

Apparently sixteenth-century French philosopher Montaigne had it right when he noted, "Nothing fixes a thing so intensely in the memory as the wish to forget it." Continually trying to "perish the thought" may not be such a good approach after all.

Sometimes Willpower Is All We've Got

As we strive to live righteous lives, every available safeguard against sin is required at different times and to varying degrees. There will be times when our willpower is all that stands between us and sin.

Certainly we are never better off sinning than using willpower to resist sin. But neither should we consider willpower a perfect solution. The spiritual safety afforded by willpower is not unlike the physical protection provided by guardrails along the side of a road. We would never want to drive on a dangerous stretch of mountain highway without a guardrail. At the same time, we wouldn't want to rely only on the guardrail to keep us on the road. We would also want to drive carefully and keep the car well maintained so our contact with the guardrails could be kept to a minimum.

In a similar way, our willpower may at times be all that stands between us and sin. Yet we'd be wise to also develop other means of protecting ourselves so that we have every part of our armor against sin.

Submitting to God's Will Instead

We can claim that we resist sin for good, religious reasons. Since "the natural man is an enemy to God" (Mosiah 3:19), we may feel that it's proper to resist our natural tendencies. It may come as a surprise to us, but the solution proposed in the scriptures for dealing with our natural tendencies is very different—even the opposite—of white-knuckled resistance and forceful control.

Certainly the virtues of resistance are extolled in the scriptures—but not the kind of forceful resistance we often resort to. In fact, when we are told in the Bible to "resist the devil," that advice is coupled with the priority that we "submit to God." (James 4:7.)

Submission is commended in the Book of Mormon as well. We are told to "[*yield*] to the enticings of the Holy Spirit . . . and [become] as a child." (Mosiah 3:19; emphasis added.) We also learn that "sanctification cometh because of . . . *yielding* [our] hearts unto God." (Hel. 3:35; emphasis added.) Far from being ambitious, strong-willed, and "in charge" of their lives, Alma advised his people to be "humble, and be submissive and gentle; easy to be entreated; full of patience and long-suffering; being temperate in all things; being diligent in keeping the commandments of God at all times; asking for whatsoever things ye stand in need, both spiritual and temporal; always returning thanks unto God for whatsoever things ye do receive." (Alma 7:23.)

Jesus Christ certainly provides the ultimate example of submission and yielding through his obedience to God's plan, which included his sacrifices in Gethsemane and Golgotha. Following his example, we should pray that God's will, not our own, be done.

The counsel to be submissive and yielding goes beyond good, general advice for living. Speaking specifically of dealing with temptation, Alma said: "Humble yourselves before the Lord, and call on his holy name, and watch and pray continually, that ye may not be tempted above that which ye can bear, and thus be led by the Holy Spirit, becoming humble, meek, submissive, patient, full of love and all long-suffering." (Alma 13:28.)

Submissive. Yielding. Humble. Gentle. Meek. Patient. Easy to be entreated. Long-suffering. Led by the Holy Spirit. Certainly not the captains of our own souls.

Going with the Grain

Mark: I remember my father's advice to me as a young child when he came into the workroom one day and found me working on a little wood project. "Whether you're sanding or sawing," he said, "go with the grain whenever you can." By following his advice, I was surprised to find that not only were the cuts cleaner and the surface of the wood smoother, but the work was actually much easier! Little did I know then that I had just learned the Taoist concept of *Wu Wei*.

In Taoist philosophy, the concept of *Wu Wei* means to go with the nature of things. It is illustrated by the following story from the writings of Chuang-tse, as told by Benjamin Hoff:

At the Gorge of Lü, the great waterfall plunges for thousands of feet, its spray visible for miles. In the churning waters below, no living creature can be seen.

One day, K'ung Fu-tse was standing at a distance from the pool's edge, when he saw an old man being tossed about in the turbulent water. He called to his disciples, and together they ran to rescue the victim. But by the time they reached the water, the old man had climbed out onto the bank and was walking along, singing to himself.

K'ung Fu-tse hurried up to him. "You would have to be a ghost to survive that," he said, "but you seem to be a man, instead. What secret power do you have?"

"Nothing special," the old man replied. "I began to learn while very young, and grew up practicing it. Now I am certain of success. I go down with the water and come up with the water. I follow it and forget myself. I survive because I don't struggle against the water's superior power. That's all."[4]

Some systems of martial arts make use of this same concept. Years of training and experience have shown the masters that it is possible to tap into their competitor's power and use it for their own purpose. Paradoxically, this is done through yielding. In judo or jujitsu, the idea is to use your opponent's strength to your advantage. You may set your opponent off balance by unexpectedly giving way, deplete his or her energy by yielding to the blows, or in a myriad of other systematic ways use agility and deliberate passivity to defeat brute strength.

Steeped in our Western tradition, we have a difficult time with this concept of going with natural forces rather than resisting them. Instead of acting in accordance with the nature of things, we desire to conquer nature, to subdue it, to control it. And when we can't, we are determined to at least fight it.

Elder Richard G. Scott of the Council of the Twelve Apostles has taught this principle:

> Once I had a measuring tape that didn't work. I decided to fix it. I began to remove the side cover plate to find what was wrong. In a few moments, I knew I was in trouble. Suddenly, the whole mechanism exploded in my hands. There were tape and spring flying in all directions. My efforts to put it all back together were frustrating and often painful. Irritated, I just about threw the whole thing away. Then I thought, "Someone designed this tape. If I can discover the principles that make it function, I can fix it." With greater patience, I began to examine the mainspring and found that if coiled in a certain way, instead of resisting and complaining, it

easily responded. Soon the spring was coiled, carefully placed in its housing, the tape joined, the cover replaced, and it worked perfectly.

So it is with you. When, through violation of God's laws, you cease to function properly, force and compulsion will not restore you. You must search out the Designer's plan. As you follow it, you will become more pliable. You can be "repaired" more easily, and you will function well again under His divine influence.[5]

Nothing magical happens when we go with the grain; we're just tapping into power that's already there for the taking. Sometimes it almost seems magical, though. That's because rather than butting heads with nature, we're actually carried along by the flow of natural forces.

If we think about it, we can see this in our lives every day. When we're learning something we love, we no longer have to force ourselves to study. When we are serving someone we love, we no longer have to write reminders on our "to do" list. The task may be very difficult, but the effort involved becomes practically irrelevant because our hearts are in the work. The difficulty no longer matters—it is eclipsed by the desires of our hearts.

The "Flow" of God

But sometimes we're afraid to go with the grain. We know that "doing what comes naturally" often creates heartache and pain as people abandon their inhibitions and behave irresponsibly.

Certainly the "natural man is an enemy to God." But remember that God's prescription for dealing with the natural man is not to resist, but to yield. Not to just yield, but to yield *unto God*. (See Mosiah 3:19.) Our goal is not indiscriminate submissiveness, but submission to the will of God. Giving up the helm is not enough—we must allow our souls to be "captained by Christ," as President Ezra Taft Benson so clearly taught.[6]

As a general, blanket statement, "just go with the flow" is not good advice—there are too many different "flows" we could go with.

Societal and personal inhibitions are necessary precisely because many of our natural tendencies must be curbed and directed. However, we must not forget that the most potent and compelling "flow" results from the power of God.

As Joseph Smith wrote, "What power shall stay the heavens? As well might man stretch forth his puny arm to stop the Missouri river in its decreed course, or to turn it up stream, as to hinder the Almighty from pouring down knowledge from heaven [or to hinder him from anything else he desires to do]." (D&C 121:33.)

What a powerful "flow" is described in this verse! We are fortunate that it is our opportunity, not to stretch forth our puny arms in an effort to resist its force, but to join with it, tapping into its power.

Tapping Into the Flow

In any effort to attain victory over self, we can do only a small part of what needs to be done. Consider David's victory over Goliath. It was not the might of David's arm that killed Goliath, nor was it some special quality of the six stones he chose. No, it was the power of the Lord. If we are to conquer our own Goliaths, then, we can't rely on our measly resources or our own energy and effort. We must depend on God.

Catherine Thomas, instructor of ancient scripture at BYU, has written with great insight: "Men were designed to be essentially powerless in this life except for their agency either to draw on God's power and become God, or to refuse his power and become something less."[7]

Designed to be powerless? That may sound like a strong statement. But haven't we received the same message from the Lord? He said: "I am the vine, ye are the branches: He that abideth in me, and I in him, the same bringeth forth much fruit: *for without me ye can do nothing.*" (John 15:5; emphasis added.)

Again, as emphasized by President Ezra Taft Benson, this power does not require aggressive action on our part, but submissive acceptance. President Benson said:

11

"In the book of Revelation is a powerful and profound invitation from the Savior. He says, 'I stand at the door, and knock: if any man hear my voice, and open the door, I will come in to him.' (Rev. 3:20.) Note that He does not say, 'I stand at the door and wait for you to knock.' He is calling, beckoning, asking that we simply open our hearts and let Him in."[8]

Divine attributes simply cannot be forced. We must open our hearts to the influence of God and "*let* [our] bowels . . . be full of charity towards all men . . . and *let* virtue garnish [our] thoughts unceasingly." Only then shall our "confidence wax strong in the presence of God" and in a consistently unforced manner, "the doctrine of the priesthood shall *distil upon [our] soul[s] as the dews from heaven.*" (D&C 121:45; emphasis added.)

As the branch receives nourishment from the vine. Like dews distilling from heaven. As we discuss this great capacity that can be tapped by submission, we are reminded again of the Eastern perspective, which is tuned to the power of yielding.

> Man is a thinking reed but his great works are done when he is not calculating and thinking. "Childlikeness" has to be restored with long years of training in the art of self-forgetfulness. When this is attained, man thinks yet he does not think. He thinks like the showers coming down from the sky; he thinks like the waves rolling on the ocean; he thinks like the stars illuminating the nightly heavens; he thinks like the green foliage shooting forth in the relaxing spring breeze. Indeed, he is the showers, the ocean, the stars, the foliage.[9]

What a difference it makes when we release ourselves to the care of the Lord and rely upon his grace. While we may have found our own willpower and strength to be insufficient, we have received assurance from God: "My grace is sufficient for all men that humble themselves before me; for if they humble themselves before me, and have faith in me, then will I make weak things become strong unto them." (Eth. 12:27.)

Setting the Sail

Perhaps, then, a key to greater self-control is not working harder but working smarter. Rather than trying to force ourselves along (white-knuckled willpower), our first goal should be to tap into the natural flow of the will of God. Then we can let that flow carry us along to where *he* wants us to be.

When it comes to changing our lives, our energy is often better spent in setting the sail than in rowing the boat.

Throughout our days, we spend most of our effort on rowing the sailboat of our lives. We spend our energy on this concern and that, worrying, working, and trying to control. In the frantic midst of all our doing, we would do well to stop rowing and instead set the sail to pick up the winds of God's power.

How? By learning his will, and then being submissive to it. By letting his power have place in us. By letting him do his work in us, rather than keeping him out while we try to do it ourselves.

When we try to conquer the problems of our lives through willpower alone, we're essentially trying to be our own saviors. When we set our sail in Christ, allowing his blessings, power, and grace to come to us, we're turning to him and letting him be our Savior.

Putting God and his will first in our lives. Letting his power direct and guide and bless us. That is setting the sail. And that's the true path to lasting and divine change.

"Conquerors" or "Sheep"?

Jesus acknowledged the need for submissiveness when he likened his disciples to sheep.

Unfortunately, "sheep" has become a derogatory label in our society, connoting thoughtless compliance and imitation. Independence is considered a trademark of the American culture. Even within the Church we encourage and foster self-reliance.

Independence and self-reliance have their place. But when we try to be independent of God, or to be self-reliant instead of reliant on God's Spirit and grace, we essentially begin to cut ourselves off from his help and blessings. We put ourselves in a position where we have little left besides willpower in our battle for change.

Yes, the Lord tells us to "come off conqueror[s]" (D&C 10:5) and to be "overcomers" (see Rev. 2:26). Yet these certainly are not admonitions to seek to triumph over sin single-handedly. Even though it may be appealing to think of ourselves as conquerors, the scriptures make it plain that we're really sheep who must be protected and healed by the shepherd.

The humanistic portrayal of man as sufficient to the tasks that face him may bring self-respect and a sense of empowerment to the human spirit. However, we go too far if we assume that God therefore has a secondary role. An overemphasis on our own power leads even those of us who understand the gospel to look to ourselves, rather than to God, in our attempts to live a better life. Then, rather than relying completely upon the merits of God when we wish to overcome our mistakes (see 2 Ne. 31:19), we assume we must pay our dues for sin by resisting temptation through the sheer energy of our own will. We seem to believe that white-knuckled resistance is somehow a necessary penance for the sins we've committed—even though such resistance can never dig us out of the pit of sin.

It is as though we are in the wilderness with the Israelites, surrounded by fiery serpents, refusing to look to the brass serpent on Moses's pole (see Numbers 21), failing to comprehend the potential for healing that Christ offers us, "because of the easiness of the way" (Alma 37:46).

We may be surprised by the infinitely greater sense of energy and empowerment that come as we look to Christ in our attempts to change. Speaking to those who are in the process of repentance, Elder Richard G. Scott offers this encouragement and witness:

> Please understand that *the way back is not as hard as it seems to you now.* Satan wants you to think that it is impossible. That is not

14

true. The Savior gave His life so that you can completely overcome the challenges you face. (See 2 Ne. 2:6–8.) . . .

Lucifer will do all in his power to keep you captive. You are familiar with his strategy. He whispers: . . . "You can't change; you have tried before and failed." "It's too late; you've gone too far." Don't let him discourage you. . . .

Your exercise of faith permits you to call upon the strength of the Lord when you need it. Obedience to His commandments allows that help to be given. The power of God will come into your life because of your faithful obedience to His commandments. . . .

Don't confront your problem armed with only your own experience, understanding, and strength. Count on the infinite power of the Lord by deciding *now* to be obedient to His teachings. (See 2 Ne. 31:19–21.) . . .

I promise you, in the name of the Lord, that He will help you. He will be there in every time of need. He gave His life so that you can change your life. I promise you that you'll feel His love, strength, and support. Trust Him completely. He is not going to make any mistakes. He knows what He is doing. . . . Be obedient to His teachings, and He will bless you. I promise you He will bless you.[10]

Some people point to their successful changes without any help from the Lord. Yet even if we are able to change our behavior on our own, we still must submit to the Savior. President Benson testified that "repentance means more than simply a reformation of behavior. Many men and women in the world demonstrate great willpower and self-discipline in overcoming bad habits and the weaknesses of the flesh. Yet at the same time they give no thought to the Master, sometimes even openly rejecting Him. Such changes of behavior, even if in a positive direction, do not constitute true repentance."[11]

Returning to our metaphor: as sheep, it is not enough for us to enter into the path of the Shepherd. In addition, we must know him, recognize his voice, and follow it implicitly. (See John 10:3–4.)

Let us not ignore what the Savior can and will do to help us change. Some amount of struggle is inevitable when we try to overcome sin. But the Good Shepherd reaches out to us with loving arms, seeking to bless us with his power and bring us unto the divine nature—which surely is the ultimate goal of all of us.

Learning to Let

If we have always tried to "take things into our own hands," how can we now place our lives in the hands of the Savior? If we are used to "praying like it's up to God and then working like it's up to us," how can we learn to rely more on him to help us do the work? In short, how can we give up some of our zeal for our own personal "mission statement" and submit our will to God's? Here are a number of suggestions you may find helpful:

1. Recognize Your Need for God. For decades, those who have suffered with problems of self-control have benefited from programs such as Alcoholics Anonymous. In AA and other "Anonymous" programs, the first three steps of overcoming addictions are (a) admitting that we are powerless—that our lives have become unmanageable, (b) believing that a power greater than ourselves can restore us to sanity, and (c) making a decision to turn our will and our lives over to the care of God. These steps are based on true principles and have firm scriptural support for Latter-day Saints.

2. Kneel to Pray. Some who are on the path of overcoming sin report that one of the most difficult steps of change is the act of kneeling to pray. Yet it is one of the most vital, since God usually doesn't reach down to help us until we exercise our agency to ask. Don't just "go through the motions" of prayer; kneel to convey an attitude of submission to your Heavenly Father.

3. Pray to Learn the Lord's Will. To some extent we are all, each in our own way, running from the Lord, "as a wild flock which fleeth from the shepherd." (Mosiah 8:21.) Aldous Huxley once said, the "third clause of the Lord's Prayer is repeated daily by millions, who have not the slightest intention of letting any will be done, except their own." After making note of Huxley's observation, author Lewis M. Andrews confides,

In my own case, I have come to rely on this excerpt from Fenelon, Archbishop of Cambrai, which I have recited every morning for almost a decade:

"Lord, I know not what to ask of thee. Thou only knowest what I need. Thou lovest me better than I know how to love myself. Father, give to thy child that which he himself knows not to ask. Smite or heal, depress me or raise me up: I adore all thy purposes without knowing them. I am silent; I offer myself up in a sacrifice; I yield myself to thee; I would have no other desire than to accomplish thy will. Teach me to pray. Pray thyself in me."[12]

4. Be Open to Making Spontaneous Changes. Instead of praying for the Lord's guidance only once or twice at set times during the day, pray on the spur of the moment at a variety of different times. Seek his guidance and be willing to break your routine by setting aside your schedule to perform some unexpected service, letting him set your priorities for the day, or questioning your knee-jerk emotional reaction to a situation.

5. Look for God's Hand in All Things. We let go of our control when we trust. Yet, as a rule, we only trust the familiar. When you were a child you probably would have been willing to jump into a swimming pool to the open arms of your parents. If, on the other hand, a stranger were to have been waiting to catch you, you likely would have hesitated.

God's influence is all around us, but he is a stranger to us unless our eyes are tuned to his influence. One way to attune our eyes (and hearts) to God's hand in our lives is to make specific note of it in our journals each day. As we make a consistent, daily effort to consider the events in our lives in this light, we will be amazed at the ways in which the Lord is touching our lives—ways that previously may have gone unnoticed.

6. Set Aside External Criteria for Success. Too often we let our happiness and success be determined by the judgments of others. And too often we spend so much time running after a particular manifestation of success that we fail to see the greater success we've already achieved.

Consider the words of Viktor Frankl, a psychiatrist who learned some of his most important lessons as a prisoner in a Nazi death camp during World War II:

> Again and again I admonish my students both in Europe and in America: "Don't aim at success—the more you aim at it and make it a target, the more you are going to miss it. For success, like happiness, cannot be pursued; it must ensue, and it only does so as the unintended side-effect of one's personal dedication to a cause greater than oneself or as the by-product of one's *surrender* to a person other than oneself. Happiness must happen, and the same holds for success: you have to *let it* happen by not caring about it. I want you to listen to what your conscience commands you to do and go on to carry it out to the best of your knowledge. Then you will live to see that in the long run—in the long run, I say!—success will follow you precisely because you had *forgotten* to think of it."[13]

With those changes that lead to success, as with all other changes, we often just have to let go!

7. Slow Down the Pace. Throughout our lives we try to force our will on things around us; forcing change through willpower is just one manifestation of a greater need for control. Hurrying through our days is a symptom of the problem: we have too little time, so we try to cram more into each day than it really ought to hold.

If we will slow down the pace, relinquishing some of our control over time, it will help us with other control issues as well. One individual reported that as soon as he released himself from getting everything done in a hurry, he felt much freer and more relaxed in general:

"I tried doing my household chores at half-speed. When I took out the garbage I had time to appreciate the cool shade from the green trees in my yard, and then on the way back to the house I noticed the snow-capped mountains against a gorgeous blue sky. As I did the dishes at a slower pace I actually found myself enjoying the time it gave me to just think. I have become more appreciative of God and have observed his hand more in the simple things I used to take for granted as I hurried off to accomplish the next task."

8. Test Your Fears of Letting Go. When we expect things to fall apart if we don't maintain a tight grip, it's understandable that we're afraid to "let go." Practice letting go of little things and see if the feared consequences actually do occur. After experimenting with letting go of her need to correct her husband, one woman was surprised to observe that "other people didn't seem to think of us as uneducated or ignorant in spite of the silly things he sometimes says."

Mark: One scorching August afternoon, I had just returned home from an afternoon of errands in a hot car with my son Ryan, then eight months old. We were both hot and grumpy. Seeking relief, I turned on the tap to the garden hose and held it while Ryan splashed in the water with his hands. Suddenly he grabbed the hose and, despite my best efforts, began to spray us with it. There I squatted, hand gripped tightly on the hose, straining to maintain my balance so that neither of us would get drenched. But disaster finally struck when Ryan pointed the hose directly at our faces. I grabbed at the hose with my eyes closed but lost my balance, and we both fell in the muddy puddle we had created on the grass. The funny thing was, now that we were both wet I finally relaxed! The tension in my muscles was gone, my worry about "what might happen" disappeared. My fear was realized and I discovered it was no big deal. We were then free to splash and play to our hearts' content!

9. Be "Willing to Be Made Willing." Just as children may rebel against the greater wisdom of their parents, we often cherish our independence instead of submitting our will to God's. In order to reach our goal of yielding, we may have to build on the slightest yearnings and desires to follow the Lord and pray for their increase. In this way, a simple "willingness to be made willing" can become a stepping stone to more complete submission.

Dean: Jim and Carla were experiencing tremendous marital problems. Complaints like "He's too critical," and "She never listens" were rampant. Divorce was on the horizon in spite of a temple marriage and four beautiful children. They both echoed, "We no longer love each other." It was apparent there had been much hurt and pain in their relationship, and their hearts had become hardened toward each other.

I counseled them to put their differences aside at least for a time and recall times when they felt more positively toward each other. I encouraged them to seek the blessing of softer hearts—which could come if they would listen to the whisperings of the Spirit. They agreed to try.

Independently, they decided to visit the grounds of the temple where they were married twenty years earlier. Carla said, "I waited until Jim left for work and the kids were on their way to school. I knelt and prayed to the Lord that my heart might be softened, that I could put past hurts behind me. I felt impressed to go to the temple grounds—not to enter the temple but to experience the environment. I felt a sense of peace come over me as I drove toward the temple. I walked around and just pondered my situation. I sat down on a bench and said to the Lord, 'I'll do what you want me to do.'"

Jim, on the way to work, had similar direction. He reported being preoccupied by the suggestion that his heart needed to be softened. He went to work and told his secretary he would return in a couple of hours. He just drove around and, without design, "ended up at the temple." He parked his car and just walked around. He tried to remember when times were good in his marriage and recalled the sweet experience of looking across the altar at Carla as they were married. For a few minutes he forgot his pain and a sense of peace came over him. He reported, "It just seemed easier to breathe. It felt like a load was being lifted. My heart was being softened." He noticed a woman sitting on a bench some distance away but didn't realize it was Carla until he was close enough to touch her.

He sat next to her, but they said very little; instead, they shared the feelings of the moment with their hearts.

They still had much work to do to repair their relationship, but a beginning had been made because they were both willing to be made willing.

From Resistance to Submission

We live in a time of unprecedented belief in human capacity. We hear that the average human uses only 7 percent of his or her brain; we see athletes surpassing previously unheard-of accomplishments; we enjoy the benefits of modern technology and science.

Surely we can be captains of our fate!

But, as we have seen, we are not—and when we try, we fail.

Amidst the throngs shouting, "We can do it," "We're doing it," "We've done it," we need to interject our own rejoinder: "Thanks and glory be to God."

We have prospered. We have many strengths and abilities. Does that mean we need God less now? Far from it. We are creatures; he is the creator. We are the clay; he is the potter. Whether we acknowledge it or not, we need God's help if we are to succeed in becoming like God.

We were surprised when one client said his terrible struggles with self-control had actually, in a way, turned out to be a blessing. "I have always felt pretty self-sufficient. It took a problem like this to teach me that I couldn't do it alone."

President Ezra Taft Benson has said, "Just as a man does not really desire food until he is hungry, so he does not desire the salvation of Christ until he knows why he needs Christ."[14]

Perhaps, then, if there is anything to be learned from our struggles with willpower, it is that we cannot do it on our own and we do need Christ. Change does not come easily or quickly. But it is possible when we rely upon him.

It is a loving Master who is knocking at the door and awaiting our invitation to enter in. Our strength may be insufficient for the tasks we face, but through the atonement he will compensate where we are deficient and then help us turn those very weaknesses into strengths. All this is possible if we will submit to him.

■ CHAPTER 2 ■

THE MOTIVATING POWER OF THE HEART

Actions of progression replace actions of self-indulgence. . . . The
compulsive cycle is not simply obliterated by repentance: it is transformed.
—MARTHA NIBLEY BECK AND JOHN C. BECK

"You Can Do Anything When Your Heart Is in It"

Every day we do difficult things with little or no reliance on willpower. Consider:

How much willpower does it take for a fly-fisherman to get up at 5:30 A.M. so he or she can get to the stream before daybreak?

How much willpower does it take for a child to run from ride to ride at an amusement park, from early in the morning until late at night?

How much willpower does it take for a group of young kids to sweep off the patio so that they can play basketball?

How much willpower does it take for a teenager to spend four focused hours preparing for the prom?

You can probably think of times in your life when you were able to do these or similar things without trying to get "psyched up" at all. If you think about it, we need rely on willpower (or *mind*-power) only to the extent that our *hearts* are not in what we're doing. Problems of self-control can be conceptualized as battles between the mind and the heart. The heart *feels* like doing one thing, but the mind *thinks* better of it. Consider the following examples:

23

"I know I should study, but I just can't bring myself to sit down and do it."

"When I get mad, I'm always sorry later about the things I said and did."

"I really want to lose weight; it's just next to impossible to discipline myself."

"I believe pornography is wrong, but I just can't control myself."

The common theme that runs through all of these statements also echoes in the words of every individual with whom we've worked on issues of self-control. Notice how, in each sentence, it almost sounds as though the speakers are talking about two separate "selves," or at least two different parts of themselves. There is a "self," for instance, that recognizes the importance of studying and a "self" that cannot be brought to sit down and do it. There is a "self" that wants to lose weight, and a "self" that is impossible to discipline.

These two different selves are what we refer to as the *mind* and the *heart*. (We'll talk later about the differences between them and the way each tends to operate.) When we understand correctly, we see that to one degree or another our heart is central to our problems of self-control. If that were not the case, we could simply leave our problems behind us like a snake sloughing off its dried and useless old skin. Instead, those problems cling to us despite all our willpower and self-control.

We lack self-control because our hearts and minds can't agree on what we're trying to do. One way to bring them to agreement is to find another, higher motivation, something that will engage your heart so thoroughly it will supersede the bad habit or attitude you're trying to control.

One way we invite our clients to explore the other motivations in their lives is to have them ask themselves, When I am no longer pouring energy into my problem, where will that energy be going instead? When I am no longer engaging in the behavior I am trying to control, what will I be doing instead?

24

When you are no longer engaging in the behavior you are trying to control, what will you be doing instead?

This is an important question—one we must answer if we wish to replace destructive motivations and desires with those of righteousness and joy. We can state our goals in negatives: "I don't want to waste my time on video games anymore." "I want to stop masturbating." "I need to stop destroying things when I get angry." Or, "I've got to start abstaining from drugs and alcohol." Those statements only describe what we don't want. The next question then has to be: "So what will I do *instead?*"

What will we do instead? That question is ripe with possibilities. What means enough to us that we are willing to let it be a ruling principle in our lives? What means more than the bad habits or attitudes we're trying so hard to eliminate?

To help us better understand this process of finding new motivations of the heart, let's explore a couple of case-studies in change.

The People of Ammon

One of the amazing conversion stories in the scriptures is the story of King Lamoni and his people, who became known as the people of Ammon. The story is striking in large part because of the radical change in their very nature. This is some case of "before" and "after"!

First, consider the "before" picture: The wicked disposition of the people is described in Alma 17:

"[They were a] wild and a hardened and a ferocious people; a people who delighted in murdering the Nephites, and robbing and plundering them; and their hearts were set upon riches, or upon gold and silver, and precious stones; yet they sought to obtain these things by murdering and plundering, that they might not labor for them with their own hands.

"Thus they were a very indolent people, many of whom did worship idols, and the curse of God had fallen upon them because of the traditions of their fathers." (Alma 17:14–15.)

25

These people were so bad, Mosiah himself was reluctant to let his sons go among them to preach! Yet the sons of Mosiah themselves knew what they were getting into: "They supposed that great was the work which they had undertaken. And assuredly it was great." (Alma 17:13–14.) Not only did these Lamanites have the weight of their own evil choices to overcome, but they had the evil traditions of their fathers as well.

As a result of the preaching of Ammon, however, the hearts of the people were changed by the Spirit of God. First, Lamoni was overcome by the Spirit and lay for a time as though he were dead. When he rose, he expressed the joy of his conversion and fell to the earth again. Then his wife and servants were likewise overcome by the Spirit and fell to the earth as well. Once they rose again, "they did all declare unto the people the selfsame thing—that their hearts had been changed; that they had no more desire to do evil." (Alma 19:33.)

This conversion was more than a process of being *intellectually* convinced of the truth of the gospel. Rather, the *hearts* of these wild, hardened, ferocious, and indolent people had been completely changed—they had no more desire to do evil.

This change in the people of Ammon is truly remarkable—the evil aspects of their nature had literally been removed from their beings. But what replaced that evil? When the people of Ammon stopped murdering, robbing, plundering, and worshiping idols, what did they do instead? Alma answers this question by saying: "Ammon did . . . teach them all things concerning things pertaining to righteousness. . . . And they gave heed unto his word, and they were zealous for keeping the commandments of God." (Alma 21:23.)

Before their conversion, these people were not indifferent. They were completely immersed in a destructive and repulsive way of life— "zealously" involved in their evil ways. But following their conversion, Alma describes them as "zealous for keeping the commandments of God."

Alma later describes some of the changes in their behavior with more specificity:

"They became a righteous people; they did lay down the weapons of their rebellion, that they did not fight against God any more, neither against any of their brethren. . . .

"And they began to be a very industrious people; yea, and they were friendly with the Nephites; therefore, they did open a correspondence with them." (Alma 23:7, 18.)

To say that they changed their approach to social relationships is an understatement. They were no longer aggressive but became friendly with those who had formerly been their enemies. Their work habits changed as well. Whereas they had previously been "indolent," now they were "very industrious."

One final, interesting point illustrated by this case is the enduring nature of their change: "As many as were brought to the knowledge of the truth, . . . and were converted unto the Lord, never did fall away." (Alma 23:6.) What a wonderful transformation these people experienced! Their destructive nature was not merely removed, it was permanently replaced. Previously they had been consistently motivated to do evil, but now they were compelled by a passion, a "zeal," for righteousness.

The Case of Ken

As counselors, we have seen many people change from fighting the problems in their life to earnestly, even passionately, pursuing positive alternatives. When this transformation occurs, it seems as though the individual's previous problems are transcended—it's not so much that they have gone away, but they have shrunk in importance against the backdrop of a newfound sense of enthusiasm for a new fresh purpose in life.

The case of Ken illustrates such a transformation. For Ken, the problem of self-control revolved around school and studying (though, of course, the principles of his change apply to many other kinds of problems as well). When Ken first went to college, his heart just wasn't in his schoolwork.

"I'd try to buckle-down and stay disciplined, but I'd end up swinging from one extreme to the other—one week studying, the next week playing. Sometimes I'd take off with my friends for the week and we'd totally forget about school. But after a few days I'd feel terrible, and I knew I had to get back to work if I was going to have any chance of passing my classes."

When Ken finally began to gain control, it wasn't simply through greater willpower. Instead, the real change began when he decided to pursue as a major an area he truly loved—travel and tourism:

"When I first came to college, it was just to get a degree. I didn't know what I wanted to do, so I accepted my dad's goal for me: pharmacy. But I hated all the chemistry classes, and I just couldn't get motivated. Now I've found my niche in life—and I'm getting straight A's in the process!"

Previously, he had always seen schoolwork and time with other people as two mutually exclusive activities. Now he found a way to combine them.

"It's not that I overcame the pull in either direction; it's that there's just not that huge conflict anymore. More and more I'm finding that balance between tasks and people because I'm combining the two: working, but working with people. It feels fantastic."

While Ken is spending even more time and energy on schoolwork now, it has actually become "easier" than it was before. Not only is schoolwork less of a burden, but he finds previous "time-wasting" activities less appealing.

"Now I only spend maybe an hour out of a day "playing." That's good—you have to give yourself a chance to have fun and relax. But now I don't have to feel guilty about wasting an entire week without anything to show for it. I don't want to paint a picture that everything's perfect—sometimes I still make bad choices about how I spend my time. But it's just not the kind of problem it used to be, the kind that engulfs your life."

The change in Ken's life obviously did not begin and end as a career choice only. It also involved his perception of himself and his relationship with God as well: "I like the person I see—this person that God has told me I am, the person my patriarchal blessing tells me that I am, the person other people have told me I am. I've never believed those things about myself before."

Not surprisingly, Ken's new passion for life lights up his entire countenance.

"People who knew me six months ago hardly recognize me. Yesterday one friend said, 'I can't believe how happy you are now. And you seem to have more energy than ever!' I loved hearing that. I used to try to hide the hurt, the stress, the pressures of my life, but now I don't feel I'm trying to hide anything. I might start tearing myself down but not nearly as much any more. Now if I start comparing myself to someone else, it doesn't linger even ten minutes. I feel like there's no stopping me now."

As we interviewed Ken, his excitement and hope were contagious! His passion and enthusiasm for a positive purpose in life have almost completely displaced the negative cycle of self-denial and self-indulgence in which he was previously immersed.

With these case studies in our minds, let's look more closely at ways we can become motivated for good with all our hearts. We can find the power to change when we (a) find a purpose outside ourselves, (b) become "anxiously engaged," (c) displace bad in our lives with good, and (d) develop a clarity of purpose. Let's talk about each of these.

Finding a Purpose outside Ourselves

Abraham Maslow was a psychologist who devoted his career to exploring what led to fulfillment in life. (This emphasis strongly contrasted with that of most other psychologists, who study pathology and dysfunction.) Pursuing the question of just what potential humans have, he studied healthy, strong, creative people—people he referred to as "self-actualized." He describes one of his most significant findings:

"Self-actualizing people are, without one single exception, involved in a cause outside their own skin, in something outside of themselves. They are devoted, working at something, something which is very precious to them—some calling or vocation in the old sense, the priestly sense. They are working at something which fate has called them to somehow and which they work at and which they love, so that the work-joy dichotomy in them disappears."[1]

To find something to which we can devote ourselves wholeheartedly is to discover meaning that transcends our own existence—something outside ourselves. Ironically, problems of self-control usually amount to exactly the opposite—they are completely *inside* ourselves, inside our own skin. We sit alone watching TV. We indulge in a petty emotional tirade, a fit of temper that benefits no one and only serves to relieve our own tension. We seek release of a sexual urge by engaging in solitary fantasy or any of a number of illicit sexual acts. We gorge on food to placate internal pain that remains private and hidden. Finding the kind of immense, transcendent purpose we are describing in this chapter can help us overcome the small, insignificant internal concerns that sometimes keep us mired in our problems of self-control.

Genuine involvement with others is a vital key to transcending self-centeredness. We have observed that almost everyone who gains greater self-control becomes more involved with others in the process. Connections and synergy with others bring a zest for life that we often may not feel in isolation. This sense of excitement and fulfillment can turn out to be the solid gold for which our problems of self-control served as miserable counterfeits.

For many, however, becoming more involved with others in meaningful ways is not as simple as it may sound. Difficulty in making positive connections is often what leads in the first place to other, less adaptive attempts to feel good. Remember, then, that learning to make connections is part of a process, and it may take time. Still, it is profitable to watch for ways to make heartfelt connections. It may feel risky and awkward at first, but the process will surely expand your purpose and enlarge your soul.

As we search for a purpose outside ourselves, let us remember that our most worthwhile efforts will be devoted to the cause of Christ. President Ezra Taft Benson described this as being "*consumed in Christ*." People who are consumed in Christ

> set fire in others because they are on fire. . . .
>
> Their will is swallowed up in His will. (See John 5:30.)
>
> They do always those things that please the Lord. (See John 8:29.)
>
> Not only would they die for the Lord, but more important they want to live for Him.
>
> Enter their homes, and the pictures on their walls, the books on their shelves, the music in the air, their words and acts reveal them as Christians.
>
> They stand as witnesses of God at all times, and in all things, and in all places. (See Mosiah 18:9.)
>
> They have Christ on their minds, as they look unto Him in every thought. (See D&C 6:36.)
>
> They have Christ in their hearts as their affections are placed on Him forever. (See Alma 37:36.)
>
> Almost every week they partake of the sacrament and witness anew to their Eternal Father that they are willing to take upon them the name of His Son, always remember him, and keep His commandments. (See Moro. 4:3.)
>
> In Book of Mormon language, they "feast upon the words of Christ" (2 Ne. 32:3), "talk of Christ" (2 Ne. 25:26), "rejoice in Christ" (2 Ne. 25:26), "are made alive in Christ" (2 Ne. 25:25), and "glory in [their] Jesus" (see 2 Ne. 33:6).
>
> In short, they lose themselves in the Lord, and find eternal life. (See Luke 17:33.)[2]

Becoming "Anxiously Engaged"

In section 58 of the Doctrine and Covenants, we are warned that it is not pleasing for us to be commanded in all our good works. Rather than taking a "slothful," inactive approach, we are commanded that "men should be anxiously engaged in a good cause, and do many things of their own free will, and bring to pass much righteousness." (D&C 58:27.)

Surely being "anxiously engaged" does not mean we should approach our lives in an overly careful, worried manner. We suspect that the Lord was using the word *anxious* to mean "eager" or "urgent." The word *engaged* can mean everything from "involved" or "committed" to "captivated," "enchanted," "fascinated," "interested," "engrossed," "immersed," "absorbed," "enthralled," "gripped," or "intrigued." Let's experiment with some alternative ways of expressing this command:

Men should be urgently engrossed in a good cause.

Men should by eagerly immersed in a good cause.

Men should be enthusiastically absorbed in a good cause.

Clearly, this scripture tells us much more than just to go beyond what we're commanded. We should find good work we're intrigued by—good work that touches and motivates us personally, something we can be enthusiastic about, that we might do it "of our own free will."

Free will is different from willpower. Maslow noted that self-actualized people don't have to "grit [their] teeth and squeeze" in order to do good. Instead, they become involved so passionately in the activity that it seems to carry them along.

> Self-actualization means experiencing fully, vividly, selflessly, with full concentration and total absorption. It means experiencing without . . . self-consciousness. . . . At this moment of experiencing, the person is wholly and fully human. This is a self-actualizing moment. This is a moment when the self is actualizing itself. As individuals, we all experience such moments occasionally. . . . We can help [others] experience them more often. We can encourage them to become totally absorbed in something and to forget their poses and their defenses and their shyness—to go at it "whole hog." From the outside, we can see that this can be a very sweet moment. . . . We can see the recovery of some of the guilelessness of childhood; some of the innocence and sweetness of the face can come back as they devote themselves fully to a moment and throw themselves fully into the experiencing of it. The key word for this is "selflessly."[3]

When we are keeping commandments out of sheer willpower, we are not anxiously engaged. We may be willingly involved, or even grudgingly participating, but we are not anxiously engaged. The key is desire—when our true desires are engaged, we won't need so much willpower; and we'll be doing things the way the Lord would have us do them.

Displacing Bad with Good

In one test of creativity, subjects are faced with the following problem: A ping pong ball has fallen to the bottom of a tube that stands, in a vertical position, fastened permanently to the floor. Some participants try, unsuccessfully, to reach into the tube and retrieve the ball with tools that are provided. The problem is that some tools are not long enough to reach the ball, while others are too wide to fit into the tube. Some subjects eventually give up in exasperation, but others discover a creative solution, realizing that water can be poured into the tube. The water displaces the air in the tube, and the ball pops to the surface, rising higher each time water is poured in. Once water fills the tube, the ball is easily retrieved.[4]

In the same way, one of the best methods to remove something from our lives is to displace it with something else. As the case of Ken illustrates, we can become so caught up in a purpose for good that we simply have less time and energy to get wrapped up in the bad.

Alma the Younger and Paul the apostle both utilized this principle. At one point, each had strong desires to tear down the Church, then repented. In their repentance, they permanently replaced bad with good. It would be absurd to imagine that after they were converted they had to resolve each morning, "I just have to resist the temptation to preach against Christ today." Instead, they had become captivated and eager to build up the Church and had thrown themselves completely into the cause of Christ.

The story of the Birdman of Alcatraz provides another striking illustration. After numerous violent crimes, he was doomed to a life in prison. For months he lived a mean, narrow, pitiful existence. His hate festered and anger continued to dominate his life.

Then one day a sign of hope and life came into the desolate environment of his cinder-block cell: a tiny, injured bird fluttered in. The helpless creature somehow touched a seed of compassion within the inmate, and he began to care for it, nursing it back to health. A capacity to nurture and love began to sprout and take root within him. Another bird came to rest at his window. He fed it and it returned. Soon he was talking about his birds with other inmates. He learned to control his temper and relate more agreeably with the guards—at first to gain favors for his birds but more genuinely as time went on.

More birds came and he gradually built up a small aviary in his cell. When some of his birds began to die, he learned everything he could about bird diseases. He experimented with treatments and found those that worked. He learned to write more effectively so he could communicate his passion for his birds. He published articles about his methods of caring for them, corresponded with a woman who was a fellow bird-lover, and even developed a relationship with her that resulted in her visiting the prison.

As his story unfolds it becomes clear that the more time he spent with his birds, the more human he became. While this is a tragic story, in a sense, it is also a story of great hope. The changes in the Birdman demonstrate how even the simplest of positive purposes can swell to displace what is destructive in our lives.

Certainly it is true that good can displace the bad in our lives. When we are deeply involved in a positive purpose, our souls, and even our bodies it seems, resonate with the power and energy of God. Just as precious ore that has been purged of imperfections is more pure, we are more fully ourselves when we are in the midst of doing good rather than evil. In essence, the process of gaining more self-control and increasing in righteousness is not one of changing *from* who we are. Rather, we are changing *to* who we are. Changing is a process of becoming more fully ourselves.

Developing a Clarity of Purpose

The more clear our purpose, the more we'll be able to be motivated with all our hearts.

Steve DeVore has spent years studying high achievers. He has also overcome tremendous hurdles in his own life, not the least of which was learning to walk again after a debilitating bout with polio. He notes: "The main characteristic of historical as well as contemporary high achievers is what we call 'sensory orientation.' . . . If you ask them to explain to you their goals, their hopes, their aspirations, they would be able to do this in three-dimensional sensory detail. They would be able to paint a picture for you with their words."[5]

Viktor Frankl had much to say about finding meaning and seeking purpose in one's life. In *Man's Search for Meaning* he writes about the experience of those (including himself) who were imprisoned in a German concentration camp during World War II. Frankl observed that those who survived relied frequently on a vivid vision of their present and future purpose. They found refuge from their dreadful circumstances by retreating to this "inner life."

Frankl himself clung to the image of his beloved wife. One particularly difficult morning, while engaged in the onerous labor of prison life, he had the following experience:

> We were at work in a trench. The dawn was grey around us; grey was the sky above; grey the snow in the pale light of dawn; grey the rags in which my fellow prisoners were clad, and grey their faces. I was again conversing silently with my wife, or perhaps I was struggling to find the *reason* for my sufferings, my slow dying. . . . In a last violent protest against the hopelessness of imminent death, I sensed my spirit piercing through the enveloping gloom. I felt it transcend that hopeless, meaningless world, and from somewhere I heard a victorious "Yes" in answer to my question of the existence of an ultimate purpose. At that moment a light was lit in a distant farmhouse, which stood on the horizon as if painted there, in the midst of the miserable grey of a dawning morning in Bavaria. *"Et lux in tenebris lucet"*—and the light shineth in the darkness. For hours I stood hacking at the icy ground. The guard passed by,

35

insulting me, and once again I communed with my beloved. More and more I felt that she was present, that she was with me; I had the feeling that I was able to touch her, able to stretch out my hand and grasp hers. The feeling was very strong: she was *there*.[6]

Frankl had an equally vivid vision of a future spent teaching other professionals what he learned from his experiences in the camp.

I became disgusted with the state of affairs which compelled me, daily and hourly, to think of only such trivial things. I forced my thoughts to turn to another subject. Suddenly I saw myself standing on the platform of a well-lit, warm and pleasant lecture room. In front of me sat an attentive audience on comfortable upholstered seats. I was giving a lecture on the psychology of the concentration camp! All that oppressed me at that moment became objective, seen and described from the remote view of science. By this method I succeeded somehow in rising above the situation.[7]

Incredibly, this kind of clarity of purpose provided Frankl and other prisoners with the fuel to live on. Perhaps this is the vision possessed by the high achievers described by Steve DeVore. This same clarity of purpose can provide motivation for us, even if the obstacles we face are less formidable. When our desire for a goal springs from deep within our hearts, to say that we can "almost taste it" may not be such an exaggeration after all.

Nourishing Our Passions for Good

We each have numerous desires in our life. The key is not so much to squelch the bad ones as to nourish the good. We are reminded of the words of Alma the Younger:

"I know that [God] granteth unto men according to their desire, whether it be unto death or unto life; yea, I know that he allotteth unto men, yea, decreeth unto them decrees which are unalterable, according to their wills, whether they be unto salvation or unto destruction.

"Yea, and I know that good and evil have come before all men; he that knoweth not good from evil is blameless; but he that knoweth good and evil, to him it is given according to his desires, whether he desireth good or evil, life or death, joy or remorse of conscience." (Alma 29:4–5.)

It *is* possible to stay motivated, to keep our hearts engaged in our attempts to change. But to do so, we must have an alternative that is meaningful to us—and meaningful not only in an intellectual sense but in a deeply emotional one as well. Let your vision of that positive alternative be clearer than the temptation of your old life; then you will be well on the path to change. *You can do anything when your heart is in it!*

CHAPTER 3

THE POWERFUL BUT UNRULY HEART

Our judgment of the inner voice varies between two extremes: it is regarded either as merest nonsense or else as the voice of God. That there might be a middle point worthy of consideration occurs to no one.

—C. G. JUNG

The Motivating Power of the Heart

There is in all of us a continuing tension between heart and mind. "Willpower" is often of the mind, while "motivation" is often of the heart.

One reason we must strive to develop the desires of our hearts is that actions based on rational understanding or intellectual conviction alone are difficult to maintain. As we work with individuals who struggle with self-control, over and over again they tell us that they can only go so long on the energy provided by intellectual convictions. Eventually they tend to let down and do what they "feel like" doing. On the other hand, most agree that when they are acting upon heartfelt desires, they find it easier to act consistently, without the stops and starts of behavior that is forced.

Elder Joseph B. Wirthlin has identified the heart as the seat of motivation: "Mere knowledge in itself may be, but it is not necessarily, power. Knowledge is not motivation. Neither is logic. . . . The springs of human action are inherently in the feelings, not the intellect."[1]

Ideally there would be a harmony between our hearts and our minds. However, when we have a conflict between the two, our actions and decisions generally spring from the heart. We act based on our emotional, not intellectual, responses to the world around us. The heart seems to drive us and convince us more powerfully than does the mind.

It is absurd to the rational mind to think that we would buy a certain kind of soft drink simply because the beach in the commercial is covered with more beautiful bodies, the ocean water is a deeper blue, or because the bass guitar is thumping a more catchy beat. This is absurd to the rational mind—but advertisers have long recognized that we can be motivated at a level that is deeper than logic. At times we react naively, on a purely emotional level. Otherwise, why would tobacco companies successfully spend millions of dollars on advertising pages upon which the only *written* (and therefore *intellectual*) message is a warning that the surgeon general has determined that smoking can be hazardous to your health?

> Cigarette advertisements provide an interesting example of the existence of . . . two systems. It is a matter of wonderment that advertisers are willing to spend millions of dollars to spread the message that their product can kill. Apparently, they intuitively recognize that a picture in which their product is associated with any of a variety of pleasant events, including nature scenes, liberated women who have come a long way, and ruggedly handsome men who desire to have their Luckys lit, can readily override a straightforward written appeal to reason. This makes perfect sense if it is assumed that there are two conceptual systems, one more responsive to images and emotions and the other to words and reason, and it is the former that often has the more powerful influence on behavior.[2]

The motivating power of the heart is not limited to trivial actions and decisions of everyday life. Anyone who has purchased a house will confirm that often the "feel of the place" is usually more important than such technical considerations as the results of a report by a qualified inspector. It seems that the color of the carpet often plays a larger role than the soundness of the foundation!

Similarly, many of us choose a career based on gut feelings, with little or no reliance on a logical consideration of the options or some objectively standardized career test.

Even when it comes to the most important decision of our lives—choosing a marriage partner—most of us depend more on our hearts than on our minds. Ask friends why they chose the spouse they did. Very few will answer, "Based on a methodical and rational process of elimination . . . " More likely, you'll hear, "I felt comfortable around him." "When we were together it just felt right."

Sure, some do use a checklist of criteria that must be met by a potential spouse. But this is often just an attempt to bring the mind up to speed on a decision the heart has already made. After all, notice how quickly criteria are crossed off the list as "not as important as I thought" or "no longer relevant" when the object of our affections doesn't completely match our old template.

And so it goes with the myriad of decisions, both minor and major, that we make each day. As much as we hate to admit it, we often unthinkingly pursue the desires of our hearts.

"Heart Trouble": Why We Mistrust Our Emotions

Our emotions are a powerful driving force. Unfortunately, they sometimes steer us wrong. We may fall for get-rich-quick schemes even when we know better. We may make fools of ourselves because we've "fallen in love." We may even buy a car because "it just feels right," only to later find that we've landed a real lemon. The plain and simple fact is that the heart is sometimes misguided.

Research has found that epilepsy in certain regions of the brain can lead to a partial "aha!" experience. That is, the individual experiences a sense of emotional conviction—but without an accompanying intellectual insight. Experience also teaches us that the emotional conviction accompanying a "discovery" is the same whether that discovery turns out to be true or false. Arthur Koestler notes the example of the astronomer Johannes Kepler:

All through his life Kepler hoped to prove that the motions of the planets round the sun obeyed certain musical laws, the harmonies of the spheres. When he was approaching fifty, he thought he had succeeded. The following is one of the rare instances on record of a genius describing the heady effect of a false inspiration—Kepler never discovered that he was the victim of a delusion:

"The thing which dawned on me twenty-five years ago before I had yet discovered the five perfect bodies between the heavenly orbits; which sixteen years ago . . . caused me to devote the best years of my life to astronomical studies, to join Tycho Brahe and to choose Prague as my residence—that I have, with the aid of God, who set my enthusiasm on fire and stirred in me an irrepressible desire, who kept my life and intelligence alert—that I have now at long last brought to light. Having perceived the first glimpse of dawn eight months ago, the light of day three months ago, but only a few days ago the plain sun of a most wonderful vision—nothing shall now hold me back. Yes, I give myself up to holy raving. If you forgive me, I shall rejoice. If you are angry, I shall bear it. Behold, I have cast the dice, and I am writing a book either for my contemporaries, or for posterity. It is all the same to me. It may wait a hundred years for a reader, since God has waited six thousand years for a witness."[3]

True understanding or knowledge combines intellectual belief with emotional conviction. The Lord in his revelations, whether regarding topics of a secular or spiritual nature, provides man with an emotional conviction of the truth through the conduit of our heart. However, we cannot expect this emotional conviction, this "burning in the bosom," unless we have first "studied it out in our minds." (D&C 9:8.) In addition, the Lord says, "Yea, behold, I will tell you in your mind *and* in your heart, by the Holy Ghost, which shall come upon you and which shall dwell in your heart." This means of communication, to both our mind and our heart, he then identifies as "the spirit of revelation." (D&C 8:2–3; emphasis added.)

It is dangerous to rely exclusively on our feelings. We disregard the guidance of our rational mind at our own peril. History is full of stories of people whose emotional convictions led them astray. We have all experienced incidents where what felt right, even powerfully so, turned out to be the wrong decision in retrospect. Because of the potential for misguidance, we cannot simply indulge the desires of our heart.

The Dangers of Relying Exclusively on the Heart

Some counselors urge their clients or friends to follow their hearts exclusively, abandoning the "repressive" and "moralistic" inhibitions of the rational mind. Such individuals suggest that we should "do whatever comes naturally." As M. Scott Peck warns, however, just because a desire or behavior is

> natural, does not mean it is essential or beneficial or unchangeable. . . . It is also natural to defecate in our pants and never brush our teeth. Yet we teach ourselves to do the unnatural until the unnatural becomes itself second nature. Indeed, all self-discipline might be defined as teaching ourselves to do the unnatural. Another characteristic of human nature—perhaps the one that makes us most human—is our capacity to do the unnatural, to transcend and hence transform our own nature.[4]

Mihaly Csikszentmihalyi, a professor of psychology at the University of Chicago, echoes Peck's concern. "By nature . . . we are born ignorant. Therefore should we not try to learn? Some people produce more than the usual amount of androgens and therefore become excessively aggressive. Does that mean they should freely express violence? *We cannot deny the facts of nature, but we should certainly try to improve on them.*"[5]

As you can readily tell, the best solution to a previous overreliance on the mind is not a reactionary swing to the opposite extreme. We believe that the answer is not to simply follow our hearts indiscriminately, doing whatever we feel like doing at the time.

The character Tigger in A. A. Milne's *Winnie-the-Pooh* is one who follows his heart—wherever it leads him. This gives him spontaneity and vigor, but his life of passion is not without its pitfalls—though he rarely stops to think much about them. He bounces in and out of situations, never fully completing the tasks he has started and never pausing long enough to consider that there may be a better way.

When we live like Tigger, we are not truly as "free" as we would like to believe. Csikszentmihalyi exposes the erroneous nature of thinking that would label a completely unrestrained life as "liberated":

> The problem is that it has recently become fashionable to regard whatever we feel inside as the true voice of nature speaking. The only authority many people trust today is instinct. If something feels good, if it is natural and spontaneous, then it must be right. But when we follow the suggestions of genetic and social instructions without question we relinquish the control of consciousness and become helpless playthings of impersonal forces. The person who cannot resist food or alcohol, or whose mind is constantly focused on sex, is not free to direct his or her psychic energy. . . .
>
> Submission to genetic programming can become quite dangerous, because it leaves us helpless. A person who cannot override genetic instructions when necessary is always vulnerable. Instead of deciding how to act in terms of personal goals, he has to surrender to the things that his body has been programmed (or misprogrammed) to do. One must particularly achieve control over instinctual drives to achieve a healthy independence of society, for as long as we respond predictably to what feels good and what feels bad, it is easy for others to exploit our preferences for their own ends.[6]

Thus we see, freedom from reason is not freedom at all. To be truly effective and fulfilled in life, we must cultivate and follow both the mind and the heart.

Stalemate between the Heart and Mind

James clearly taught how essential it is that we have internal unity. "A double minded man is unstable in all his ways," he wrote. (James 1:8.)

In the story of Dr. Doolittle, the doctor receives as a gift a strange animal—the push-me-pull-you. Rather than a head at one end and a tail at the other, the push-me-pull-you has two heads, one at each end of its body. The push-me-pull-you was a real crowd-pleaser, a wonderful novelty. In the real world, however, the push-me-pull-you would not survive for long. Whenever the intentions of the animal's two minds conflicted, its body would be pulled in opposite directions. The end result would likely be stalemate, neither head getting what it wanted.

When the powerful mind and the even more powerful heart are in conflict, we may find ourselves in a predicament much like that of the push-me-pull-you. Consider the description, shared with us by psychotherapist Allen Gundry, of one individual who struggled with a problem of self-control:

"In one therapy session, in the middle of the worst time for me, my therapist asked me to describe an image that represented what I was going though. I told him I felt like I was a dog stuck in the middle of a bridge. On one side were my family and friends and the Church and everything that went along with them. On the other side was my problem and all its temptations. And I felt like I, as this dog, was being pulled in both directions. I couldn't decide which way I should go because either way I would be giving up too much—both options were intolerable in some way. I didn't see any way out. I felt like the pressure would just continue to build. Either I would get pulled apart, the bridge would crumble, or the water would rise and wash me over into the stream, but there was no positive resolution possible."

When the rules of the mind and the desires of the heart collide, sometimes one or the other "wins out." Often, however, neither side is fulfilled. Then, rather than progressing toward either goal, the individual remains stuck somewhere in between. Rather than doing what we feel like doing or what we think we should do, we do neither. We remain lukewarm. We stay on the fence.

Often, when the heart and the mind become locked in battle, neither one truly wins.

Consider a simple example. We *feel* like going out and playing with friends. We *think* we ought to stay in and do homework. We end up doing neither, spending the evening in front of the TV with a textbook in our lap instead. In the end, we have not accomplished any studying, and we feel guilty for it. Yet we haven't enjoyed the release of tension from indulging in fun either, and we feel a pang of regret over that missed opportunity. We truly are left with the worst of both worlds.

It seems that Nathaniel Branden was describing people in this state when he said, "The senseless tragedy of their lives is that [they] betrayed their mind, not for the sake of gratifying some violent if irrational passion, but for the sake of indulging meaningless or senseless whims that they can no longer remember."[7]

Like some push-me-pull-you, we find it difficult to act in one way or another when there is conflict between our hearts and our heads. We cannot drag ourselves very far in one direction before we find ourselves being tugged in the other.

But, take courage, there is an answer beyond stalemate. We believe there is good news for those who have a difficult time acting against the desires of their hearts. We believe that true self-control transcends both self-indulgence and self-denial. In short, we believe that the Lord does not wish us to drag our hearts, kicking and screaming, into a life of submission to the mind. No, there is a better way—it is to bring both mind and heart to submission to the Lord.

The Lord Requires Our Hearts

"The Lord requireth the heart and a willing mind." (D&C 64:34.) Most of us already know how to give God our minds, at least in large part—it's often the mind that gets us up and off to church on Sunday morning, and it's the mind that usually causes us to resist temptation. But what about our hearts?

In spite of the potential for misguidance and the dangers of self-indulgence, we must work to rehabilitate the desires of our hearts rather than just repressing or trying to rid ourselves of them. The Lord does not want us to obey him based exclusively on willpower. Rather, he wants us to "follow [him], with full purpose of heart." (2 Ne. 31:13.)

"I, the Lord, require the hearts of the children of men." (D&C 64:22; emphasis added.)

Instead of judging us based on our intellectual comprehension exclusively, instead of requiring only obedience of the mind, the Lord is immensely interested in the desires of our hearts. The first great commandment is that we love the Lord, not only with our mind, but with all our heart as well. (See Matt. 22:37.) Similarly, when we serve him, we are told to perform our service with all our hearts, as well as our minds. (See D&C 4:2.)

Even actions that appear righteous from the outside are unacceptable when they are not driven by our hearts' desires.[8] When compliance is forced, even by our own minds, we do not reap the same blessings as we do from obedience that springs from the desires of our hearts. In the words of David O. McKay: "Mere compliance with the word of the Lord, without a corresponding inward desire, will avail but little. Indeed, such outward actions and pretending phrases may disclose hypocrisy, a sin that Jesus most vehemently condemned."[9]

Likewise, Joseph Smith once wrote: "Remember God sees the secret springs of human action, and knows the hearts of all living. . . . It is also useless to make great pretensions when the heart is not right before God, for God looks at the heart."[10]

Rather than obeying only because we think we should, the Lord wants us to obey willingly, because we truly want to. "But this I say, He which soweth sparingly shall reap also sparingly; and he which soweth bountifully shall reap also bountifully. Every man according as he purposeth in his heart, so let him give; not grudgingly, or of necessity: for God loveth a cheerful giver." (2 Cor. 9:6–7.)

The heart and its true desires must be enlisted in our battle against sin and habit. Unfortunately, we can't simply choose through willpower to reclaim our hearts' desires. Something much more—and much different—must be done.

PART TWO

RECLAIMING THE HEART

CHAPTER 4

TUNING IN TO THE WISDOM OF YOUR HEART

When we understand more than we know with our minds, when we understand with our hearts, then we know that the Spirit of the Lord is working upon us.

—HAROLD B. LEE

Imagination is more important than knowledge.

—ALBERT EINSTEIN

Our Hearts Need Reclaiming

In the preceding pages we've tried to show that when we seek to change, we must go beyond simply resisting our evil desires. We must learn to pursue good with all our hearts so that willpower is no longer necessary.

Hopefully, we may someday reach the point where all our desires are righteous. Then the Lord will trust us without reservation, as he did Nephi, the son of Helaman. Here are the Lord's words to him:

"Blessed art thou, Nephi, for those things which thou hast done; for I have beheld how thou hast with unwearyingness declared the word, which I have given unto thee, unto this people. And thou hast not feared them, and hast not sought thine own life, but hast sought my will, and to keep my commandments.

"And now, because thou hast done this with such unwearyingness, behold, I will bless thee forever; and I will make thee mighty in word and in deed, in faith and in works; yea, even that all things shall be done unto thee according to thy word, for thou shalt not ask that which is contrary to my will." (Hel. 10:4–5.)

What an accomplishment it would be to know that all our hearts' desires are in line with the will of the Lord. On the other hand, we know that because of the fall, our inclination is in the direction of evil rather than good. (See Eth. 3:2.) In fact, it is possible for the desires of our hearts to deteriorate to the point that "every imagination of the thoughts of [the] heart [is] only evil continually." (Gen. 6:5.)

Most of us fall somewhere between Nephi, whose desires were all righteous, and the people of Noah's time, whose desires were all evil. In this position, we are faced with a challenging dilemma: How do we resist the desires of our hearts that have been directed toward evil without also losing the tremendous motivating strength of those desires? How do we tap into the unequaled power of the heart as a driving force for good without allowing evil desires to reign as well?

For most of us, if we wish to develop our ability to live whole-heartedly for good, we must reclaim and rehabilitate the desires of our hearts, not simply follow them. First, we must begin to tune in to the wisdom of our hearts, nourish the good we find, and develop our ability to express it. We must discipline the heart, with the help of the Lord. And we must allow the Lord to change our unworthy desires from bad to good. We will talk about all these things in the chapters that follow.

To begin with, how do we go about tuning in?

The Case of Scott

> Mark: The case of Scott, a client I worked with, demonstrates the lack of energy and motivation we feel when we're cut off from the positive powers of our hearts. He came to therapy seeking help in his struggle to control his urges for pornography.

50

"I have these lofty goals: I want to succeed as an artist, I hope to get through graduate school, and I want to be admired for what I've accomplished. I feel like I've been blessed with talents, and I feel a responsibility to live up to my capability. I know exactly what I need to do to reach my goals, and I have a strategy.

"Last weekend I even followed through on what I'd promised myself I'd do. I had an incredibly productive weekend, got caught up in two of my classes. I always follow through according to my plan when I'm excited about it like that. But then after a couple of days, as usual, I lost my motivation."

"What do you mean, 'lost your motivation'?" I asked.

"I just couldn't do it anymore," he answered in exasperation. "I couldn't keep it up."

"What happened?"

He sighed. "Monday afternoon, instead of going to class, I went up to Salt Lake to an adult bookstore and spent two hours looking at pornographic magazines."

"It doesn't sound to me like you lost your motivation at all," I said.

"What in the world do you mean?" he asked, surprised.

"A person who is willing to get out of bed, cancel his schedule for the day, get on a bus, travel for an hour, stand for two hours, then repeat the trip back again sounds pretty motivated to me!"

He laughed. Of course he was motivated—but he was motivated in the wrong way when he sought out pornography. In addition, he was experiencing conflicting motivations: his drive for discipline and success clashed with his desire to let down his inhibitions, relax, and even look at pornography. Over the weekend, his more desirable motivations had won out. By Monday afternoon, however, the undesirable motivations overshadowed his more lofty goals.

"Feel Like Doing" vs. "Think I Should Do"

I suggested to Scott that he seemed to be having a battle between his mind and his heart. His heart seemed to "take over" at times when he "indulged" and did things he felt like doing. On the other hand, his mind was in charge when he was "disciplined" and did the kinds of things he thought he should do.

Scott had labeled the things he felt like doing as "bad" and the things he thought he should do as "good." To a real extent, he was justified in doing so. "Let your conscience be your guide" is probably a better motto than "Allow yourself to be carried along by your whims and urges." But Scott's complete denial of his feelings was sapping his energy and motivation.

"Perhaps, Scott, in your quest for self-discipline, you have come too far," I suggested.

"Too far?" he laughed. "I'm not nearly disciplined enough."

"Of course, the problem is not that you've come too far in being in complete, intellectual control of your life. No, you've come too far from the desires of your heart. I suspect you have some legitimate desires that you've been abusing through pornography."

As we talked about specific examples from his life, he admitted that he always tried to subjugate what he felt like doing to what he thought he should do.

"It hasn't always been that way," I said. "Remember when you were a kid? When you felt like playing you went out and played. When you felt like running you ran. When you felt like splashing in mud puddles, you did.

"But eventually, what you felt like doing has caused you enough trouble that you have come to mistrust your gut feelings, your inclinations. I believe, though, that there is a sweet baby somewhere in that dirty bathwater of what you feel like doing. Some good can come from listening to your heart, and you're missing out on that good as you try to avoid the bad."

Respecting the Wisdom of Your Heart

One key to overcoming our mistrust of the heart lies in recognizing the tremendous wisdom that is accessible to our hearts but not our minds. In our culture we prize intellectual analysis. Logic. Reason. "Be rational about it," we may advise, deriding actions that are based on emotions as capricious and whimsical. In the words of Robert Ornstein: "We deemphasize and even devalue the arational, nonverbal modes of consciousness. Much formal education consists predominantly of 'readin', 'ritin', and 'rithmetic,' and we are taught precious little about our emotions, our bodies, our intuitive capabilities."[1]

Ornstein further points out that our culture is dominated, and hence limited, by the scientific paradigm: "An impersonal, objective, scientific approach, with its exclusive emphasis on logic and analysis, makes it difficult for most of us even to conceive of a psychology that could be based on the existence of another intuitive, 'gestalt' mode of thought."[2]

Unfortunately, because of this cultural bias, most of us tend to live our lives relying primarily on our intellect, oblivious to much of the untapped wisdom that could be ours.

Consider the disciples who traveled with Christ on the road to Emmaus following his resurrection. With all their capacities for reason and logic, they did not recognize that it was Christ with whom they walked. In retrospect, however, after their "eyes were opened" (Luke 24:31), they understood that it was the Savior and immediately recalled that their hearts had comprehended his presence on a deeper level: "Did not our heart burn within us, while he talked with us by the way?" (Luke 24:32).

In other scriptures as well, true understanding is often linked with the heart. Rather than simply being "open-minded," King Benjamin counsels us to open our hearts as well. "Open your ears that ye may hear, and *your hearts that ye may understand,* and your minds that the mysteries of God may be unfolded to your view." (Mosiah 2:9; emphasis added.) Although the word *understanding* is frequently used to denote intellectual comprehension, there is evidence that understanding of the heart may be comprehension of a different kind. Jesus pointed out that we can learn something intellectually but fail to be convinced because we lack an understanding of the heart.

"And in [those who did not understand his parables] is fulfilled the prophecy of Esaias, which saith, By hearing ye shall hear, and shall not understand; and seeing ye shall see, and shall not perceive:

"For this people's heart is waxed gross, and their ears are dull of hearing, and their eyes they have closed; lest at any time they should see with their eyes, and hear with their ears, and should understand with their heart, and should be converted, and I should heal them." (Matt. 13:14–15.)

The apostle Paul certainly recognized that there are gifts and feelings of the heart that transcend knowledge and intellectual thinking. He wrote:

"[I pray] unto the Father . . .

"That he would grant you . . . to be strengthened with might by his Spirit in the inner man;

"That Christ may dwell in your hearts by faith; that ye, being rooted and grounded in love,

"May be able to comprehend with all saints what is the breadth, and length, and depth, and height;

"And to know the love of Christ, *which passeth knowledge,* that ye might be filled with all the fulness of God." (Eph. 3:14, 16–19; emphasis added.)

If we wish to follow the path the Lord has laid out for us, we must be willing to faithfully follow the righteous desires of our hearts, even when others may deride our actions as irrational. For example, of those who criticized faithful actions of the Mormon pioneers, President Gordon B. Hinckley has observed: "Wearing the spectacles of humanism, they fail to realize that spiritual emotions, with recognition of the influence of the Holy Spirit, had as much to do with the actions of our forebears as did the processes of the mind. They have failed to realize that religion is as much concerned with the heart as it is with the intellect."[3]

Our hearts, then, can apprehend wisdom unavailable to our minds. Let us learn once again to respect our intuition, our emotions, and our gut reactions to events and recognize their potential to guide us for good. And then let us tune in to the wisdom of our hearts.

Reconsidering the Messages from the Heart

At the end of the session described in the beginning of this chapter, Mark gave Scott the following chart:

Mind's Goals	Heart's Goals

Scott was instructed to pay attention to his thoughts and feelings during the week. When he *felt* like doing something, he was to write that activity in the column labeled "Heart's Goals." When he *understood* or *thought* he should do something, he was to record that behavior in the "Mind's Goals" column.

When he returned the following week, here's how Scott had filled out his form:

55

Mind's Goals	Heart's Goals
Do homework	Relax and "do nothing"
Organize finances	Sleep
"To do" lists	See movies
Go jogging	Travel
	Spend time with friends
	Look at pornography

What impact did acknowledging the "goals of his heart" have on Scott? Here's what he reported:

"It's been a long time since I paid serious attention to what I feel like doing. I'm so used to writing everything I'm *supposed* to do in my planner, then feeling guilty if I miss one little thing because I stopped to play around. Thursday afternoon, some of my roommates invited me to go play soccer and Frisbee at the park. I had blocked out the time to study, so of course I said 'no' even though I felt like going. Later, when I had 'jogging' written in my schedule, I didn't feel like going at all. I tried to force myself to do it anyway, but I just sat and watched TV instead.

"I didn't see the irony until I filled out the form that night. I had to laugh. Of course I then realized I would have been better off just going to the park with my friends and studying later, but I was trying to stick to this rigid schedule. It was funny because I even caught myself saying, 'But running after a Frisbee isn't a cardiovascular work-out.' Like sitting in front of the TV is!"

It was challenging for Scott to pay more attention to what he felt like doing, rather than trying to focus solely on what he thought he should do. Apparently, he had previously been so quick to judge all of his desires as wrong that he had simply stopped tuning in to his heart.

Try Tuning In, for a Change

Try the same exercise for yourself. On the form that follows, list the activities you *think* you should do under "Mind's Goals." List the activities you *feel* like doing in the column entitled "Heart's Goals." This form can be carried with you and filled out throughout a given day, or you may wish to fill it out while reflecting on the previous day or week. If you have a hard time coming up with items for the list, just think of a typical day and list, in one column or the other, everything you do from the time you wake up in the morning to the time you go to sleep at night.

Mind's Goals	Heart's Goals
_____	_____
_____	_____
_____	_____
_____	_____
_____	_____
_____	_____
_____	_____
_____	_____
_____	_____
_____	_____
_____	_____
_____	_____
_____	_____
_____	_____
_____	_____

Doing this exercise may well mark the beginning of tuning in to the wisdom of your heart. Of course, recognizing our desires does not mean we abandon ourselves to their control. When we listen to our hearts we only open ourselves up to more options. We can then evaluate those options, choosing those that remain consistent with our best interests. However, by tuning in again to our hearts, we discover that many of our desires are positive and healthy, though sometimes slightly different from the goals of our minds. And we discover that unworthy desires often reflect legitimate needs. Therefore, if we open our minds to the desires of our hearts, we can become more well-rounded, more balanced, and more healthy in the way we live.

Listening to Your Heart

Some of us have come to rely so much on our minds that we have lost touch with our hearts. Here's how one college student put it:

> Long ago I lost touch with my body—my brain became separated from my body, and started commanding it. My body turned into just a machine for transporting my brain around from place to place to talk unfeelingly and analytically with other detached brains. I was glad it was a big and efficient machine—but I thought it was the inferior part of me, and that my brain should be in charge and call the tune for my feelings, letting the "positive" ones out and keeping the "negative" ones safely tucked in. . . .
>
> But now I feel lost in that head, out of phase with people—and somehow I want to reach them and my own guts—to know what I really feel, and stop all these precious intellectual games—to really live and not just exist—So what do I do now?[4]

We do well when we're dissatisfied with a mind-only approach to life—God often speaks in the language of the heart. James E. Faust has said that "the heart is the seat of the emotions and a conduit for revelation."[5] If we wish to tap its true potential to apprehend wisdom from God, we must learn to listen to—or perhaps more accurately, *listen through*—our hearts. In addition to paying more attention to what you feel, as you have done in the above exercise, here are a number of other suggestions you may wish to experiment with:

1. Pray from the Heart. Frequently we offer intellectual, rather than heartfelt, prayers. We focus primarily on words, which are the language of the mind. The heart, on the other hand, communicates in emotions and visual images. The following prayer of Alma was certainly not an intellectual exercise: "Alma labored much in the spirit, wrestling with God in mighty prayer, that he would pour out his Spirit upon the people." (Alma 8:10.)

Patricia Holland points out that the words most often used to describe urgent prayer are *wrestle, plead, cry,* and *hunger.*[6] These words certainly describe a prayer of the heart, not of the mind. In their efforts to pray from the heart, some have found it helpful to follow these suggestions from Sister Holland:

> Do we really picture an actual father when we pray? Do we think of him—do we *truly* think of Him—as our Father? Do we spend any time on our knees trying to picture the being to whom we pray? May I suggest a process that works for me. I don't mean it to be a ritual for anyone, just encouragement.
>
> Find a private place and kneel comfortably and calmly in the center of the room. For a few moments say nothing, just think of him. Just kneel there and feel the closeness of his presence, his warmth, his peace. With humility, express your gratitude for every blessing, every good thing you enjoy. Share with him your problems and fears. Talk to him about each one and pause long enough to receive his counsel.[7]

2. Recognize the Spirit in Your Life. The Spirit does not speak to us only regarding "spiritual" matters. He will manifest himself in a multitude of quiet ways in our lives. And when he speaks, most often it is to our hearts and minds, not to either of them alone.

In an epistle to the Galatians, the apostle Paul identified the fruits of the Spirit as *love, joy, peace, longsuffering, gentleness, goodness, faith, meekness,* and *temperance.* (See Gal. 5:22–23.) If these are the effects of the Spirit, we can measure these attributes in our hearts as a gauge of the Spirit in our lives and as a guide for our behavior.

*When do you feel **peace** in your life? What kinds of things are you thinking and doing at those times?*

*When do you feel **love** in your life? What kinds of things are you thinking and doing at those times?*

*When do you feel **joy** in your life? What kinds of things are you thinking and doing at those times?*

*When do you feel **gentleness** in your life? What kinds of things are you thinking and doing at those times?*

We know that the Spirit cannot dwell where there is any unclean thing. By tuning in to our hearts we can recognize—and expand—the impact of the Spirit on the way we feel.

3. Feel the Love of God.

Dean: One evening at a fireside, I asked for a volunteer to help me illustrate the power of personalizing God's love. Carol, who was sitting in the front row, willingly came to the front of the room and stood beside me. I asked her to read aloud from the gospel of John, chapter three, verse sixteen, contemplating the meaning of this scripture as she did so:

"For God so loved the world, that he gave his only begotten Son, that whosoever believeth in him should not perish, but have everlasting life."

When I asked her to comment on the scripture, she said she knew that God did and does love us and that the gift of his Son is the greatest evidence of that love. Her testimony was quiet, sincere, and was reinforced by a feeling of peace that the Spirit conveyed to the hearts of those in the room.

I then asked her to recite the scripture again, substituting the word "me" in place of "the world," as follows:

*"For God so loved **me**, that he gave his only begotten Son, that if I believe in him, I should not perish, but have everlasting life."*

As she recited this revised version of the scripture, her voice began trembling at the word "me." She paused and tears came to her eyes. She finished the verse with some effort, tears streaming down her face by the final word.

Understanding, on an intellectual level, that God is a gracious and loving being is quite different from feeling—truly experiencing—that love for ourselves. When we only believe in his love (as opposed to feeling it), it is easy to exempt ourselves from its reach. Kevin, who has struggled with feelings of homosexual attraction for years, described it this way:

"I felt like the feelings I had made me unworthy to even pray. When I prayed I would almost apologize for praying, for my unworthiness. I felt like I was a bad person and God had too many good people to worry about and that my prayers weren't worth listening to. I thought God looked down on me for being the way I was."

Far from intellectual enlightenment, it was an emotional experience that made the difference for Kevin:

"I have always felt a deep desire to serve God. At the same time, though, I questioned whether I should keep trying to be good and risk failing again and again, or whether I should just give up and give in to a life that was more fitting to the kind of person I thought I was.

"One night when I was ready to give up, I prayed about it. 'Are my goals out of reach? Can I make any kind of contribution? Does the Lord need me or even want me?' I had prayed about it before, but this time I wasn't going to stop until I received an answer. I just had to know. I sat there in a chair in the living room after everyone else had gone to sleep and just went over and over my dilemma. I pleaded with God to direct me; I just couldn't see what to do on my own.

"In the middle of the night I finally got an answer. I was overcome. I felt God's love for me stronger than I had ever felt anything in my life. The peace I felt is indescribable, and I knew everything would be all right if I tried to serve him. I think for the first time I felt like I wasn't a horrible person and that God really loved me and cared about what happened to me."

Certainly Kevin knew that he had to align his life to God's will—but finally he also knew that he was not inherently evil and that with God's help he could have a lifestyle that would please him.

There are a variety of other means for obtaining an increased feeling of God's love. One individual retreats to nature to appreciate and feel a part of the grandeur of God's creations. For another, reading the description of the love one felt from the Lord during a near-death experience was a life-changing event.[8] Finally, one woman reports that singing to herself the hymn "Count Your Blessings"[9] and contemplating everything the Lord has done for her is a fail-safe method of reminding herself of his love.

4. Tune In to the Emotional Message of the Scriptures. The intellect processes information very quickly. For example, we may read a chapter in the scriptures, logically comprehending the ideas therein, in just a minute or two. We may even pride ourselves on the number of times we've "gotten through" all the scriptures.

But those who are no longer touched by the word of God are said to be "past feeling"—it is not their intellect that has failed them, but their hearts. We all know people who can "Bible-bash" with the best of them, but don't seem to truly "feel" the deep significance of the words they summarily recite. If we wish to grasp the meaning the Lord intended in the scriptures, we must tune in by opening up our hearts.

Carol, the fireside volunteer in the story above, experienced first-hand the power of tuning in to the emotional message of the scriptures. Try likening the scriptures to yourself, as she did. Or you might experiment by visualizing the events as you read about them in the scriptures. What would it have been like to be there? Whatever approach you try, be sure to look up from the page and let the content of what you're reading register in your heart. You may even wish to take a walk, keeping a scripture in your heart as you do so, in an effort to grasp it at a deeper level.

It does take time to really "get the feel" of the metaphors, analogies, and parables in the scriptures. What does it mean in your life when the Lord says that your sins, which are "red like crimson, . . . shall be as wool"? (Isa. 1:18.) What shameful, distasteful sins have stained your life? Do you really believe that the Lord can cleanse all that taint from your life completely? When the Lord declares that your soul is "more precious than fine gold" (2 Ne. 23:12), what does that mean to you? When you feel lost in some way, can you visualize the Lord leaving the rest of his flock and coming to your aid—coming for *you*, the *one*? (See Luke 15:4.)

Try taking some time to ponder specific scriptures in your heart. Besides John 3:16, there are a number of other scriptures you may wish to consider. First, 2 Nephi 1:15:

"But behold, the Lord hath redeemed my soul from hell; I have beheld his glory, and I am encircled about eternally in the arms of his love."

Take a minute to close your eyes and imagine the Lord's loving arms around you, gently holding you, comforting you. Now consider Isaiah 53:4–5:

"Surely he hath borne our griefs, and carried our sorrows: yet we did esteem him stricken, smitten of God, and afflicted.

"But he was wounded for our transgressions, he was bruised for our iniquities: the chastisement of our peace was upon him; and with his stripes we are healed."

Do you realize that you are loved by the Lord so much that he is willing to undergo such suffering? It is his love for *you* that provided the reason and the motivation to do so.

Sometime, when you feel like you can't do it on your own, open your heart to the message of Mosiah 24:13–15:

And it came to pass that the voice of the Lord came to them in their afflictions, saying: Lift up your heads and be of good comfort, for I know of the covenant which ye have made unto me; and I will covenant with my people and deliver them out of bondage.

And I will also ease the burdens which are put upon your shoulders, that even you cannot feel them upon your backs, even while you are in bondage; and this will I do that ye may stand as witnesses for me hereafter, and that ye may know of a surety that I, the Lord God, do visit my people in their afflictions.

And now it came to pass that the burdens which were laid upon Alma and his brethren were made light; yea, the Lord did strengthen them that they could bear up their burdens with ease, and they did submit cheerfully and with patience to all the will of the Lord.

If the Lord can lift the physical burdens of Alma and his brethren, surely he can lift the burdens in your life, whatever they may be. Can you picture him reaching down and removing some of the weight that you are experiencing in your life? At times we may feel that such help is unavailable to us. Then it may be helpful to feel the meaning of Romans 8:38–39:

"Neither death, nor life, nor angels, nor principalities, nor powers, nor things present, nor things to come, nor height, nor depth, nor any other creature, shall be able to separate us from the love of God, which is in Christ Jesus our Lord."

The possibilities are as broad as the scriptures themselves. The Lord can help us lie down in green pastures and lead us beside the still waters (see Psalm 23); he is there to heal our wounds and cleanse our lives. He stands knocking, and we must simply open our lives to his influence through the scriptures. Here is a story of one individual's experience using this approach to scripture study:

Dean: Kay was the victim of abuse as a child. As she tried to put her life back together, she often found it hard to read the scriptures. I suggested that she might want to tune into the message of the scriptures by visualizing them. Later she related the following:

"As I pondered the scriptures in 2 Nephi 4:33, where it talks about being encircled around in the robe of the Lord's righteousness, I began to feel the Spirit differently. One evening as I was struggling with painful memories, I found a quiet place to sit. I recalled the protection that I felt earlier as I visualized being encircled by the robes of the Lord's righteousness. As my heart reached out for comfort, I recalled images of my Primary days. I remembered pictures of the Lord blessing little children. How I longed for a blessing. What would it be like to be blessed by the Savior? What joy it must have been! I remember so vividly feeling a hand on my head. Tears began to flow. My heart was full as I felt my burdens being lifted. I had felt the Master's touch."

The peace in Kay's life was evident in her voice as she recalled tuning in to the heartfelt message of the scriptures and feeling the Lord's love for her.

As you try to open up your heart to the scriptures, be careful: You may be deceived into viewing your scripture time as less "productive" than it once was. The mind measures the success of scripture study by quantity—by pages and chapters and checkmarks on a chart. Remember, you are more concerned with quality—the extent to which you feel the Spirit and the feelings of love and faith that are growing within you.

5. Enjoy Good Music. While the written and spoken word sometimes have their roots in the mind, music and song emanate from the heart. The Lord commends music as a holy means of expression. "For my soul delighteth in the song of the heart; yea, the song of the righteous is a prayer unto me, and it shall be answered with a blessing upon their heads." (D&C 25:12.)

Our songs of praise are not only to be those which are somber and serious. He would have us express cheerfulness and enthusiasm as well: "If thou art merry, praise the Lord with singing, with music, with dancing, and with a prayer of praise and thanksgiving. If thou art sorrowful, call on the Lord thy God with supplication, that your souls may be joyful." (D&C 136:28–29.)

The power of music to energize and inspire is unsurpassed. Of course, it can also pollute our hearts and minds with unwanted thoughts and motivations. As we strive to listen to our hearts, we must pay attention to the impact of music.

6. Heed the Whisperings of Your Heart. When we approach life rationally we gather all relevant information, consider every potential outcome, weigh our options intellectually—noting the costs and bene-fits of each—and finally decide upon the action that appears most rea-sonable given "the facts."

On the other hand, when we listen to our hearts we may pay more attention to the "big picture," not becoming too wrapped up in the details. We respond based on a holistic "feel" of events and circum-stances rather than on their dissection and microanalysis.

We're not asking you to act without gathering any information or without deliberating the consequences of your behavior. However, you may find it profitable to experiment by paying more attention to what your heart is telling you. What happens when you follow your "vibes"? What happens when you don't? One individual, Chris, reported the fol-lowing:

"As I thought more about the value of my heart as a guide, I real-ized that in some ways I've been listening to my heart all along. I used to get irritated at myself because I couldn't explain why I married Pat—I just did it because it 'felt right.' Now that doesn't seem as foolish as it once did. Maybe I could sense, in my heart, compatibility in a way that wasn't rational or even describable in words. But what I sensed was real—we are compatible and we've had a long, successful marriage.

"Now I'm not so afraid to admit that I made a hiring decision at work based on a 'gut feeling' or to call up a friend on the spur of the moment because I felt like he or she needs someone to talk to. Before, I belittled those decisions as 'irrational.' I now recognize the value of my feelings as a guide, though I still try to balance them with an intel-lectual understanding so that I'm not controlled by my prejudices.

"It's funny because we have to make many important decisions in life based on incomplete information. If you use only your head to make decisions, that will drive you crazy. If you can act on faith, it's not such a big problem."

7. Pay More Attention to Relationships. We often create lengthy "to do" lists under the direction of our rational minds. While the items on those lists may seem urgent at the time, our hearts may perceive needs and motivate us to actions that are far more important in the long run. People we work with in counseling frequently tell us of listening to their hearts and being redirected from "tasks" to "people."

Have you ever responded to a feeling that you should call a friend or family member—only to be told that you were the answer to a prayer? Perhaps there was a need for a listening ear, a friendly voice, or special counsel. It may not seem logical to take time away from worldly responsibilities and achievements in order to nurture our relationships with family and friends, but in our hearts we are reminded of what really matters.

> Dean: I was an eager graduate student who wanted to get through my program as quickly as possible. I was single and could devote as much time as needed to my studies. On occasion I called my mother just to talk. We did not have a particularly close relationship when I was younger, but I sensed that she wanted that closeness now.
>
> During one of our infrequent telephone calls, I felt that she wanted me to travel across the country to spend time with her. It made no sense financially—I would have to borrow the money. I didn't feel like I had the time because I was in the middle of collecting data for my dissertation. Listening to my heart was a real battle because my mind had other plans.
>
> I traveled home and spent the summer with Mother. It was probably the best experience I had ever had with her. Little did I know it would be my last visit with her—she died shortly thereafter. I am so grateful now that I followed the "impractical" promptings of my heart.

8. Calm the Storm. Another way you can experiment with tuning in to your heart is to specifically focus on "calming the storm" of intellectual turmoil and just pondering a situation or decision from an emotional vantage point.

Some have found the following exercise helpful for quieting their thoughts and allowing themselves to just feel:

Find a peaceful environment—either indoors or out.

Relax. Allow the tension to drain from your body. You may choose to focus on your breathing. Notice how it slows and deepens as you become more relaxed.

Adopt a passive attitude. The mind is used to being very active, to "running the show," so to speak. Instead, allow your mind to sit in the audience for a change, observing what thoughts come and go. By no means do we recommend turning over the stage to unworthy thoughts. But you should refuse to engage the usual concerns and worries that sometimes seem to dominate every waking moment.

As thoughts come into your mind, simply allow them to drift in and out again at their own pace, like a cloud drifting into your vision, across the sky, and then out of sight again. You may be surprised at how easily some previously overwhelming thoughts drift away—once you no longer choose to engage them and dwell on them.

This is by no means the only way to "calm the storm" of your thoughts and tune in to feelings. One individual found it helpful to envision the Savior saying "peace, be still" to her mind with its worries and concerns, as he did to the storm at sea. (See Mark 4:39.) Another found it helpful to imagine himself turning off his thoughts as though he were turning off a water tap. Others simply repeat to themselves, "that's not helpful now" and turn attention away from intrusive thoughts.

At first blush, some of these techniques of turning from mind to heart sound too simple to work. That is what we thought when we first learned about them and tried them. Nevertheless, they have proven effective in coping with the furious mental activity that sometimes invades our peace like a flurry of irritating insects.

Whatever the method you use, turning from your thoughts to your feelings can allow you to tap into the wisdom of the heart and learn wisdom that would otherwise be out of reach.

■ CHAPTER 5 ■

NOURISHING THE GOOD IN YOUR HEART

Self-love, my liege, is not so vile a sin
    As self-neglecting.

—WILLIAM SHAKESPEARE

Built-in Needs

Our Father in heaven sent us to this earth to fulfill a number of vital purposes. In order to propel us on toward meeting those goals, he planted within us certain emotions, urges, drives, passions, impulses, and cravings. These include physical drives, such as for food and sex. These drives also include more complex desires: a craving for acceptance and support from others, a need to protect ourselves and those we love, a wish to be involved with and helpful to others. We also have deep underlying needs for growth and development—for self-improvement.

As we go from day to day, we don't stop and think about the possibilities and logically determine which needs we'll seek to fill that day. Far from experiencing these needs on a primarily intellectual level, we experience them on an emotional, and even physical, "gut" level. Hence, we frequently refer to them in the language of the physical—as "tingles," "throbs," "gnawings," "shocks," "chills," "twinges," and "pangs."[1]

We feel a rush of energy and our senses seem to be heightened as

69

we make an important, personal discovery. We gain ineffable, almost bodily, satisfaction from intimate emotional connection with others. A surge of physical energy propels us to "fight" or "flee" when we find ourselves threatened. Sexual excitement enlivens our entire body.

The Goodness of Your Heart

The word *passion* is commonly used to refer to these states of bodily readiness and physical arousal. Many religions view passions as inherently evil and base, seeing them as unique to this physical realm. When we die, it is assumed, we will be free from their tyrannical grip. From this perspective, God is not subject in any way to such emotional states.

In LDS theology, however, we know God to be a physical being. We understand him to possess body, parts, and passions. As Elder Bruce R. McConkie explained, "A God without passions cannot exist, for he would neither love his children, hate their evil ways, or be importuned by their pleas for mercy; he would sit tranquilly by, being neither moved nor affected by any occurrence, reacting neither to good or evil, and hence able to bestow no rewards and impose no penalties."[2]

We understand God to have passions, and we know this earth life to be a time of preparation, a time during which we can become more like God. Gaining a body is a part of this process. Unlike many other Christians, we understand the reception of a body to be an advancement from our previous, spirit-only existence.

Even within our LDS culture, however, we sometimes downplay the important role our passions play in our experience here on the earth. Perhaps we become confused, living as we do in a culture of extremes. It is popular to either worship passions or to label them as disgusting.

Yet, if we hope to be like God, we must be like him in passions as well. Would we desire to be like God except for this one particular? Would we prefer a body with parts, but no passions? No! Parley P. Pratt taught:

> Some persons have supposed that our natural affections were the results of a fallen and corrupt nature, and that they are "*carnal,*

70

sensual, and *devilish*," and therefore ought to be resisted, subdued, or overcome as so many evils which prevent our perfection, or progress in the spiritual life. In short, that they should be greatly subdued in this world, and in the world to come entirely done away. And even our intelligence also. . . .

So far from this being the case, our natural affections are planted in us by the Spirit of God, for a wise purpose; and they are the very main-springs of life and happiness—they are the cement of all virtuous and heavenly society—they are the essence of charity, or love; and therefore never fail, but endure forever.

There is not a more pure and holy principle in existence than the affections which glow in the bosom of a virtuous man for his companion; for his parents, brothers, sisters and children. . . .

These pure affections are inspired in our bosoms, and interwoven with our nature by an all-wise and benevolent being, who rejoices in the happiness and welfare of his creatures. All his revelations to man, touching this subject, are calculated to approve, encourage, and strengthen these emotions, and to increase and perfect them; that man, enlightened and taught of God, may be more free, more social, cheerful, happy, kind, familiar, and lovely than he was before, that he may fill all the relationships of life, and act in every sphere of usefulness with a greater energy, and with a readier mind, and a more willing heart. . . .

What then is sinful? I answer, our unnatural passions and affections, or in other words the abuse, the perversion, the unlawful indulgence of that which is otherwise good. Sodom was not destroyed for their natural affections, but for the want of it. They had perverted all their affections, and had given place to that which was unnatural, and contrary to nature. Thus they had lost those holy and pure principles of virtue and love which were calculated to preserve and exalt mankind; and were overwhelmed in all manner of corruption, and also hatred towards those who were good.[3]

Passions are an indispensable component of our physical bodies. We must learn to manage these passions, not suppress or rid ourselves of them. In Alma 38:12, for instance, we are told to "bridle [our] passions." Truman G. Madsen explored the meaning of this scripture when he wrote: "Focus on the word 'bridle.' What is a bridle for? To kill, to diminish, or even to limit the spirit and power of the steed?

Never. . . . We are given our bodies and our emotions not to destroy but to ride. They magnify our feelings and increase enjoyments. The body is a step up in the scale of progression. Indeed all that is in the earth has been given for the 'blessing and benefit of man.'"⁴

This concept is explained further in the Book of Mormon manual prepared for Institute of Religion students:

> When we learned that we would come to earth and gain a phys-
> ical body, we shouted for joy that we should be so privileged. (See
> Job 38:7.) The body is not a thing of evil, something to be ashamed
> of, and yet a great many sins are fed by the passions and desires of
> the physical temples in which we dwell. Nor should one think only
> of sexual passions and appetites in this regard. Though the sins
> stemming from such desires are grievous and devastating, there are
> other passions and needs that can lead us into trouble. For example,
> the apostle James used the same imagery of the bridle as did Alma,
> but James was speaking of the tongue. (See James 3:1–5.) We may
> grow irritable when the body is tired or speak harshly when we are
> frustrated. And do not selfishness and greed often come from our
> need to clothe, feed, and shelter ourselves? There is no evil in the
> needs themselves, only in the uncontrolled, ungoverned, or, to use
> Alma's word, the *unbridled* need.⁵

Of course, some desires are for evil rather than good. The scriptures point out that it is possible to "love darkness rather than light." (D&C 10:21.) Sometimes, it seems, rather than running for shelter we "[flee] from the shepherd." (Mosiah 8:21.) However, in order to truly reclaim the power inherent in the desires of our heart, we must begin by recognizing that at the core our desires and passions are potentially healthy, productive, and good. So how do we go about separating the good from the bad?

Pulling the Baby from the Bathwater

Remember Scott, whom we talked about in the previous chapter? Some of his desires—for example, for pornography—were wrong. But he had come to devalue all activities he felt like doing, even taking time to relax and be with others. He had lumped almost everything that didn't lead to outward progress or accomplishment (the goals of his mind) as "immature," "unacceptable," "lacking direction," "lazy," or "unrighteous."

In order to help Scott reclaim his heart's wisdom and its potential as a motivator for good, we asked him to begin to look at the potential advantages of his spontaneous side. In fact, we asked him to record both the "problems" and "benefits" that resulted each time he followed his mind and each time he followed his heart.

After a week, he returned with this observation: "I've always been well aware of the hazards of following my heart. But now I'm seeing there are problems associated with pursuing the goals of my mind as well." He showed us what he had recorded:

Benefits from Mind's Goals	Benefits from Heart's Goals
Get homework done	Find rest and relaxation
Keep finances organized	Enjoy things of life
Accomplish "To do" lists	Have time with friends
Feel productive	Have fun
Feel in control	Find sexual release
Resulting Problems	**Resulting Problems**
Feel loneliness	Miss class
Have constant fatigue	Feel lazy—and guilty
Feel "uptight"	Lack direction
	Feel immature
	Feel out of control
	May be criticized

Then Scott added: "As I continued to think about it, I noticed that the goals of my heart seem to be attempts to solve the problems that result from pursuing the goals of my mind, and vice versa! When I'm feeling lazy and guilty because I've wasted the afternoon relaxing, I make up "to-do" lists and focus intensely on getting things done—on accomplishments. On the other hand, when I'm burned-out and lonely, having spent too much time with my nose to the grindstone, I'll sleep in too late, blow off a day of school and go out of town with my friends, or look at pornography. Then the guilt and shame catch up with me and I start the cycle all over again."

Previously, Scott had always resisted what he felt like doing for as long as he could. Often that meant that his desires would build in intensity until they "took over." He would usually end up indulging on the spur of the moment, without any conscious thought or planning.

An amazing thing happened once he began to see his heart as a potential source of wisdom and evaluate some of those "goals of his heart" in a more positive light. He began to plan into his day ways for meeting those goals, doing it when he was relaxed and thinking clearly, rather than in the heat of the moment when he was in need of an escape or release. As a result, he chose more and more to meet his needs in ways that were more "healthy" and fulfilling than pornography.

Scott had begun to see that what he felt like doing may not be all bad. His life did not have to be a constant exercise in self-denial. Once he began to see his spontaneous side as having some redeeming value, he became less self-critical and more relaxed. Before, he had interpreted inconsistencies in his behavior as evidence of weakness; now he saw the value in operating in different "modes" and developing and expressing different aspects of himself. Even though he still didn't like to be "bulled over" by his desires, he saw his heart as a potential source of good.

Try It for Yourself

Take the list of "Mind's Goals" and "Heart's Goals" that you created earlier. Either throughout the day or week, or while considering a given day in retrospect, list on the top half of the "Costs and Benefits List" any benefits of pursuing those goals. Then list on the bottom half of the form the problems or costs that result from pursuing those goals.

Costs and Benefits List

Benefits from Mind's Goals

Benefits from Heart's Goals

_____

_____

_____

_____

_____

_____

Resulting Problems

Resulting Problems

_____

_____

_____

_____

_____

_____

Striking a Balance

Having filled out the "Costs and Benefits List," you will now be able to evaluate each activity on your "Goals" list (from chapter 4). Considering the costs and benefits of the various activities will likely help you make better decisions with regard to self-control. Here is a true example:

Tim complained of decreased motivation and productivity in his work. He worked out of his home and was his own boss. Business had been good for the first eight years of his marriage but had recently seemed to "hit the skids." Tim sought therapy for help overcoming some "bad habits" that had been affecting his work and were beginning to take a toll on his income, his self-concept, and his relationship with his wife. These ranged from "spending too much time worrying about little things I can't do anything about" to "watching TV when I should be working." In our initial interview he summed up his problem this way: "Sometimes these meaningless activities are all I feel I can do. I've lost my lust for life. I feel like I'm expending all the energy I can muster but it's not having any effect on my circumstances. It feels like I'm pushing against a brick wall."

Following several weeks of work on his problems, he began to have new respect for the desires of his heart. He decided to spend time relaxing with his wife in the evenings. He also took more opportunities to play and watch basketball, a sport he enjoyed immensely but had pushed out of his life as he gained more and more "responsibilities." By listing and then consciously evaluating the costs and benefits of his desires, he discovered that time together with his wife and playing basketball had none of the negative effects of brooding over the unchangeable or watching TV.

Tim gradually began to nourish and expand these more positive outlets of his heart's desires. He found that by taking time regularly to have fun in positive ways, he prevented what he called an "enjoyment vacuum" in his life, which previously seemed to add force to his temptations. The temptation to do unacceptable things came less frequently once he stopped fighting his desires and tried to fulfill them in more acceptable ways.

Most people don't see a link between their problem of self-control and other, less compelling, and usually more benign desires of their hearts. As the example of Tim illustrates, however, it seems that pursuing smaller and more immediate goals of the heart can reduce the pull of temptation in related areas. Conversely, it seems that the more we attempt to deny smaller and more immediate desires, the more we are compelled to engage in behaviors that bring us problems. For instance, if Tim watches a basketball game when he feels like it, he has met some of his needs for tension release and relaxation. But if he denies those needs, they linger on and may serve only to fuel his problem of self-control.

Most of us, like Scott and Tim, have a hard time seeing the desires of our heart as "goals." They seem more like whims, hankerings, or indulgences. But frequently our desires really are attempts, however misguided, to meet certain legitimate needs—or, as Scott said, to solve certain problems. When we see them as such, we, like Scott and Tim, will be able to begin meeting our needs and solving our problems in more appropriate ways, rather than denying them or indulging them completely.

Interestingly, Tim also used the exercises to evaluate the goals of his mind. At the top of his list of things he "should" do, he had written "organize the business finances." The biggest energy drain for him was to focus on billing and bookkeeping. Worrying about that part of his business dominated his time—but he was basically untrained in that area, and he hated it so much he wasted a lot of time at it. On the other hand, advertising and meeting contacts for his business was also something he knew he should do—and these were tasks he enjoyed and was good at. Unfortunately, he had come to focus more and more on bookkeeping—which he hated—and less and less on what he liked and was good at.

As a result of these insights, Tim decided to hire Brian, an accountant friend, to help him manage his finances. It was a real load off his mind, and gradually he turned all his accounting worries over to Brian—which left Tim free to focus on the more pleasurable aspects of his job.

The Three Levels of Mind and Heart

Our discussions with clients like Tim have led us to conceptualize three different levels of goals and activities of the heart and mind.

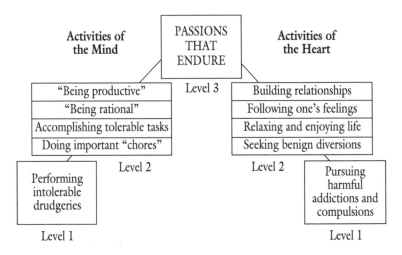

At Level 3 there is true balance between the goals of the heart and the goals of the mind. Passions that endure are activities that are important *and* enjoyable. The specific activities may not endure into eternity, but the thoughts and feelings underlying them will.

Tim's time with his wife in the evening fits the description of passions that endure. He feels that his family is his number one priority, and he takes his responsibilities with them very seriously. At the same time, the effort he puts into his relationship with his wife is rewarding and exciting. He thoroughly enjoys talking to her at the end of the day about how the day went for each of them. Advertising and networking with other professionals also fits the Level 3 category of passions that endure. Tim is enthusiastic about this part of his work, and it helps his business thrive.

Most of us are not able to spend most of our time operating at Level 3. We all spend a certain amount of time involved in activities in which there is only a partial overlap between what we feel like doing and what we think we should do. Level 2 includes all activities where there is at least partial overlap between the goals of our hearts and the goals of our minds. Those activities that are primarily mind-driven include everything from "important chores" to "tolerable tasks." We value these activities as important, and they're not completely devoid of heartfelt involvement, but we find them less enjoyable than passions that endure.

Following time spent engaged in mind-driven activities at Level 2, we are often attracted to heart-driven Level 2 activities. After a week of work and self-discipline, we want to enjoy ourselves. These include activities like relaxation and enjoyment in ways that are fairly consistent with—but not driven by—the goals of our mind. We relax and recreate, realizing that not every hour of the day, every day of the week has to be completely "productive." We switch from a mind-driven mode to a heart-driven mode. Level 2 activities also include benign diversions—these don't directly move us closer to any goals of the mind, but they don't take us further from them, either. They may indirectly facilitate productivity, however, as they provide us "downtime" to refuel and regroup.

Many of the people we work with seek counseling out of frustration because their lives are no longer operating at either Level 2 or 3. Instead, they spend most of their time at Level 1, vacillating between intolerable drudgeries and harmful addictions and compulsions.

This was the case for Tim. He spent much of his time kicking himself for not managing his finances better and telling himself he'd better get with it. He would block out an entire Saturday "to catch up and pay the price for my laziness" of the previous week. While his intentions were always good, the time he actually spent never came close to matching the twelve to fourteen hours he had set aside to organize his business. Instead, he would spend time watching TV or sitting at his desk shuffling papers and worrying.

As Tim described his situation, it sounded to us as though he engaged in intolerable drudgeries almost as a penance for his lack of productivity. He felt that he didn't deserve to enjoy himself, so he never gave himself a break. At least he didn't plan on his schedule to take a break. Instead, it was as though breaks took him! His energy would deplete and he would find himself in a stalemate, sitting idly, meeting neither the goals of his heart nor the goals of his mind.

Tim recognized that he was spending too much time engaged in harmful addictions and compulsions. In spite of that realization, he was unsuccessful in trying to resist those activities. The change came for him when he understood that the compulsions behind these Level 1 activities of the heart were directly related to his deliberate emphasis on Level 1 activities of the mind.

His objective for coming to therapy had been to develop his willpower so that he'd be able to spend more time doing distasteful chores. But his breakthrough came when he tried instead to make his behavior more consistent with Levels 2 and 3 in the activities of both his mind and heart.

The Inadequacy of Self-Denial and Self-Indulgence

The Inadequacy of Self-Denial. The desire to enjoy ourselves is not simply a desire to avoid work. It is a worthwhile desire in its own right. The problem is not in the heart itself, then, but in the pathways we sometimes choose for expressing our desires. The fact that the needs underlying many problems of self-control are real and even legitimate helps account for the inadequacy of self-denial as an exclusive means of coping with temptations.

Imagine someone becoming ill because their sole source of water is polluted. The instruction to "stop drinking that water" is certainly good advice. Ultimately, however, to be helpful, such instruction must be accompanied by guidance to a safer source of water. Without such direction, the individual will continue to drink polluted water—even harmful water seems preferable to dying of thirst!

Researchers Martha Nibley Beck and John Beck point out that even when the individual is able to resist the addictive behavior (using sheer willpower or erecting outside barriers to the problem behavior), the underlying problem that created the urge nonetheless remains. Therefore, although the addict's misguided attempt to fulfill a need has been stymied, the need remains present and unsatisfied.[6]

Unless attempts are made to meet the underlying need more effectively, resisting temptation is only a temporary solution. The feelings of urgency engendered by the need may then build and build. Or perhaps a situation may occur that highlights the need. Then temptation will be just as difficult—or perhaps more difficult—to resist than before. Again, resisting temptation has proved to be only a temporary solution if no effort is made to meet the underlying need.

The Inadequacy of Self-Indulgence. The opposite of self-control is self-indulgence, where we give in to the urge we've been trying to fight—or to a substitution that's also undesirable. This gives us fulfillment of our need, but it comes in a most unsatisfactory form—we drink the polluted water because we're thirsty, but ultimately, because it's polluted, it makes us sick.

The cycle of self-indulgence often works like this:

Step 1—We *feel* a strong need, begin to act on it, but then "*think* better of it," and stop.

Step 2—With the need unfulfilled, the desire grows.

Step 3—Later, sometimes within seconds or minutes, we give in—or we turn to some other means of trying to fill the void. We may turn to artificial productivity and "busyness," to drugs, to sexual acts or fantasies, to food, or to any number of other indirect and destructive outlets.

Step 4—Later still, we have a new urge to fill the need, but through willpower we're able to resist—temporarily. And so the cycle goes.

Lewis M. Andrews points out the role of our emotions in this cycle: "Whether we are trying to abstain from alcohol, drugs, binge eating or gambling, most failed attempts can be traced to some unexpected emotional stress. First comes the flush of anger, frustration, jealousy, or fear, then the attempt to tranquilize these negative feelings with 'just one' drink, joint, snack, or spin of the roulette wheel. In the space of minutes, the firmest resolution can slip into what seems like distant memory."[7]

One crucial key to understanding and overcoming self-control problems is tracing our impulses back to *before* the temptation to indulge. Remember, the addictive behavior is not the heart's true desire. Rather, it is usually an easier but less effective attempt to meet a need we haven't truly acknowledged—or that seems out of reach. By choosing the undesirable behavior, we often seek what seems to be an emotionally safer or easier alternative to the legitimate expression of the need. The irony is that, in the long run, the problems of self-control are actually risky, painful, and self-defeating, while giving place to our true desires can be freeing and life-giving.

The next time we experience temptation, let us refuse to get snagged in an immediate tug-of-war between resistance and indulgence. Instead, let us attempt to stay with and explore the uncomfortable feelings that immediately precede the temptation—and to find legitimate, positive, righteous ways to express them. Questions like these may help:

What am I feeling right now?

What do I want right now?

What happened just now? How did it contribute to the feelings I'm experiencing?

What would feel good right now?

Is there a way I can meet the needs I'm feeling that is not sinful?

Could there be benign—even healthy—desires of my heart that are adding force to this temptation?

If we begin to address these questions, we may begin to find alternative ways of meeting our needs, some of which will likely be more fulfilling than the ones we've been using.

Identifying More Fulfilling Ways of Meeting Your Needs

It's hard to get off the roller-coaster of self-denial and self-indulgence. We may intellectually understand the importance of avoiding either extreme and finding more positive alternatives, but how can we apply this understanding to specific day-to-day behavior and thinking? How can we know when we are on the right track? As we struggle to meet our needs in more effective ways, how can we ensure that we're not simply switching addictions to something more socially acceptable or less dangerous, but just as unfulfilling? These are questions that must be answered if we hope to follow our hearts in constructive ways. Here are eight conditions that seem to exist when our needs are being met in effective and righteous ways.

1. We are able to act more patiently, less impulsively. Feelings that prompt us to act against our own best interests are often accompanied by a sense of urgency. By contrast, when we are acting constructively, the Lord may bless us with a sense of timelessness and sweet patience. When determining whether or not to act on our feelings, it is often helpful to stay with the feeling for a while instead of deciding immediately. Don't fight the feeling or question it right away. Simply let it come. On the one hand, there is rarely a need to rush into action. On the other, if we're too quick to hush away feelings that make us uncomfortable, we may miss what they might teach us about ourselves.

As one client said: "When I was overeating, I used to avoid any thought of food. When the 'hunger' would come, I'd either eat or try to distract myself. Now I've learned to stay with that feeling—and I've learned that it's usually not about hunger, at least not physical hunger. When I allow the feeling to come and I just sit with it for a while, I can begin to uncover the underlying emotions. Sometimes it's loneliness, sometimes guilt, sometimes a sense of being overwhelmed and stressed out—like I need a break. Once I get to that level I can meet those needs in ways other than food."

Those we work with are constantly telling us, "I've discovered it's *not* about food (or drugs, or sex, or whatever) after all." When they let their feelings come they discover that those emotions lead them much deeper than the mere surface level of the symptoms. (One drug addict said, "I don't have a drug problem; I have a life problem.") By patiently working with those feelings, rather than impulsively acting on them (or squelching them), they are able to start down the path that will turn those weaknesses into strengths.

2. We're less likely to feel a continual, chronic sense of neediness. When we indulge in negative, destructive behavior, we learn to our surprise that the short-term payoff Satan promised is not a valid substitute for long-term happiness at all. Instead, we find that we have fallen for an all-around rip-off—our needs are not met very well either in the short or the long term—and, in addition, we damage our self-esteem and our ability to meet needs in other ways.

It is this rip-off, this sense of unfulfilled promise, that sometimes motivates the escalation of self-control problems. For the compulsive shopper, if spending the first one hundred dollars didn't fill the need, perhaps the second hundred will. For the alcoholic, if the first drink didn't fill the need, perhaps the second one will. For the sex-addict, if the last encounter didn't fill the need, perhaps the next one will. In the words of Jerry, one individual who was involved in compulsive sexual behavior:

"There were all kinds of problems in my relationships. I think I was trying to fill some emotional needs, but it was as though they just were not fillable. It was like a bottomless pit. No relationship was enough."

3. We're less reliant on specific behaviors or people to fill our need. Problems of self-control depend almost exclusively on specific people or specific behaviors. In the words of Stephanie, who had been involved in a lesbian relationship:

"I was a wreck. I was beat up a number of times, but I would beg my lover to come back because I was so desperate to have that feeling of emotional security. I was not safe physically, but I felt my needs were being filled. It makes me sick to think about it now, but I would have rather been beat up every two weeks than lose someone who could meet those needs. I was so desperate I would go through anything."

By contrast, when we're meeting our needs in effective ways, strength seems to come from within instead of without. We reach a point where we no longer feel a compelling need for behaviors that we find unacceptable.

4. Our lives become more varied, our personalities more multifaceted. Self-indulgence provides such a meager payoff that the only possible reason for sticking with it as long as we do is ignorance. Imagine eating a hot dog every time you're hungry simply because you're familiar with the neighborhood hot-dog stand—when there's a delicious smorgasbord waiting just around the corner.

When we are pursuing the path of maladaptive behavior, the breadth of activities we feel like engaging in becomes increasingly constricted. Food, sex, and shopping, for example, are certainly not evil in and of themselves. They have a place in everyone's life. But they are terrible ways to try to meet all our needs. Here's what two individuals had to say:

"Whenever I was discouraged or anxious—frankly, whenever I was in any kind of pain!—I would try to pacify that hurt with food. If I embarrassed myself in a social situation, I relied on food. If all I had was a lonely weekend to look forward to, I ran to the comfort of food."

"The week I heard of my sister's death, I became involved in another sexual relationship. I was in grief, but the only way I knew to express emotion, any emotion, was through sex."

Self-indulgence usually provides a very limited range of ways to meet our needs—but when we meet those needs in positive ways, we begin to experience ever-increasing subtleties of emotion and an ever-widening repertoire of responses.

For example, sexual behavior coupled with the spiritual commitment and emotional intimacy of a mature marriage relationship is fulfilling and increases in depth with sacrifice and service. Compulsive sexual behavior, on the other hand, seems the "same all the time," is more and more highly patterned, and gradually becomes less exciting. Addicts therefore seek more and more stimulation or greater and greater frequency in a futile attempt to reach the same "high" or fill the still-gaping need.

Note the findings of Martha Nibley Beck and John Beck: "The amazing thing about the several dozen active behavioral addicts we spoke with was the similarity we noticed between their personalities, despite the apparent diversity of their life-styles. After some of these people had been climbing the joy cycle for some time, the comparison was reversed: their life-styles became quite similar, and their personalities became marvelously divergent and unique."[8]

5. While the path of self-control may be difficult, it brings us to a more consistent sense of happiness. Our problems of self-control seem like shortcuts out of misery and into fleeting pleasure. But soon after engaging in those behaviors we feel disgusted and guilty. Truly growth-promoting behavior, on the other hand, is less likely to appear as a miraculous panacea. Instead, it represents the true, rocky road to joy and fulfillment. While satisfaction may not come as easily, it is maintained on a long-term basis. Again, the words of a client:

"When I was in the midst of my problem, I thought I'd always be on that emotional roller-coaster. I never thought I'd be this happy. I wish I had known then how happy I would be now. It would have made it a lot easier for me to get through the difficult times."

6. We feel no need to hide our behavior from others. When we choose unhealthy means of meeting our needs, we often do so in a solitary manner, trying not to let anyone in on our secret. Healthy means of meeting our needs, on the other hand, can be looked forward to, and even planned into our day. We can accept them as a part of our conscious, public personality. We may not flaunt those behaviors, but we would not necessarily be embarrassed or ashamed if those around us knew about them.

7. We feel closer to God. When we choose sinful and indulgent behavior as part of our lives, we not only want to hide it from others, but we also feel a sense of shame in our relationship with God. While we can truly hide nothing from God, we can avoid thinking about him, attempting thereby to free ourselves from feelings of guilt. Tragically, the real source of the guilt—our sins—remains. Therefore, we find ourselves in the position described by Alma:

"Then will our state be awful, for then we shall be condemned. For our words will condemn us, yea, all our works will condemn us; we shall not be found spotless; and our thoughts will also condemn us; and in this awful state we shall not dare to look up to our God; and we would fain be glad if we could command the rocks and the mountains to fall upon us to hide us from his presence." (Alma 12:13–14.)

8. All aspects of our lives are enhanced. We simply cannot act in a vacuum. When we indulge in maladaptive behavior, other areas of our lives are impacted in a negative way. For example, careers can suffer or be destroyed by drug abuse. Relationships may deteriorate because of angry outbursts and mistreatment. We may even become less interested in things we have always enjoyed—leisure activities, hobbies, and so forth.

On the other hand, when we're meeting our needs in effective ways, the growth spills over into other aspects of our lives. As our self-esteem improves, we care more about taking care of our health, both physically and emotionally. As our own needs are met, we become more available for spouse or friends. We become less preoccupied with veiling and propping up our own deficiencies and more able to live spontaneously in the here and now, whether with our family, at work, or in other relationships.

The Case of Barbara

The case of Barbara provides a potent example of how positive desires can be identified and nourished, and negative desires can be disciplined, in order to reclaim the heart. (Once again, we're using an example of someone with an extreme problem. Of course, the process works for all sorts of lesser challenges as well.) For years, the desires of Barbara's heart—what she felt like doing—conflicted with what she knew she should do. Specifically, she reported that for as long as she could remember she had been attracted to other females.

"My friends would talk about having a crush on this boy or that one, and while they were having crushes on guys I was having crushes on girls. I thought to myself, 'Why are you feeling these things? What's wrong with you?' I could see that my experience was just the opposite of all my friends. It was not the sexual nature of my thoughts that terrified me because I wasn't really thinking sexual thoughts at that age; it was more the differences I was beginning to recognize."

At first she merely recognized herself as different. Later she identified her feelings as homosexual and wrong.

"Later the feelings became more sexual. Faced with those feelings and the understanding that they were wrong, my approach, of course, was to deny, deny, deny and just try to keep resisting them.

"Well, I put up a good fight, but I couldn't keep it up forever. After years of denial and guilt and loneliness, I broke down and became involved in the lesbian lifestyle. It was the low point in my life in many ways, but I also felt a wonderful sense of acceptance and love from those people. They knew everything about me and they still accepted me.

"While I prized the acceptance, there were other things about the lifestyle I just couldn't tolerate. For one thing, I knew what I was doing was wrong. I was riddled with guilt, in spite of my efforts to rationalize my actions. So I would try to repent and get back in touch with my spiritual side.

"But trying to live both lifestyles was very difficult—your personality can't do that. It's very difficult to be in a lesbian lifestyle and then pull out and try to act like you're straight, or to go to church. It was just *so* intensely difficult for me; my mind couldn't deal with it. I went to church because I wanted to—I never did doubt my testimony—but I couldn't even bear to sit there because it just racked me. When I sat in church I was uncomfortable because of my lifestyle, and when I was involved in the lifestyle I was uncomfortable because I really believed in the gospel."

In the midst of this period of intense struggle and unhappiness, Barbara began to come to an understanding that her heart's desires for love and acceptance were not inherently evil after all—they had just been misapplied in a disastrous way.

"It's a huge turnaround to go from feeling vile and disgusting to feeling, 'I'm of value and Heavenly Father has a plan for me.' A lot of that turnaround came from just learning that there were real and legitimate emotional needs behind my feelings of sexual attraction. The sexual appetite is a strong one, but I learned that the power behind it is emotional. Once I knew that, I could recognize that feeling a need for attachment, acceptance, and affection was not an innately bad thing. What matters is how you go about trying to meet that need.

"I was often told, 'You're wrong for being attracted to members of the same sex; those emotions are sinful.' When I would hear those things, I'd lose my motivation to try to control my behavior. I felt I was in the depths of sin before I'd ever done a thing, simply because of this attraction that seemed to come naturally. But when I learned the truth, it gave me back control over my life. I learned, 'You *don't* always have control over who you're attracted to, but you *can* always control your thoughts and your behavior.'

"The real key was when I separated the feelings from the behavior and figured out, 'Okay, having those feelings doesn't mean you're evil. As long as you don't act on them, you can know you are a good person.' At that point I began to feel a new wholeness within myself. Finally I could say, 'I am attracted to members of the same sex *and* I'm a good person. It doesn't have to be one or the other anymore.'"

But since Barbara understood, correctly, that involvement in homosexual behavior was sinful, how could she accept and even respect her feelings of attraction to other women? The key lay in discerning the basic, unmet needs that led to those feelings. Then she could accept the feelings themselves—and she could see the potential for good in the desires of her heart.

"I had always taken my feelings of sexual attraction at face value— I just assumed that they were sexual and that was that. And since sex with other women is terribly wrong, I knew my feelings were wrong as well. I was very surprised to learn that there was actually something of value in those feelings. To my amazement, I learned that there were legitimate, righteous ways I could meet my needs for acceptance and love with other women, ways that had nothing to do with sexual involvement.

"It wasn't just the possibility of emotional intimacy that was opened up to me; it was positive physical closeness as well. It's surprising, but when you grow up with these same-sex attraction feelings you are terrified to touch someone of the same sex. You think to yourself, 'If I even brush up against a girl everybody will know I have these terrible feelings; so I will just avoid physical contact.' And yet you have these two straight girl cheerleaders holding hands and skipping down the hall, arms around each other, and they don't think a thing about it. They are filling an emotional need for physical contact in a positive and legitimate way.

"I discovered that my needs were not sexual after all. I had a need to be close, physically and emotionally, to other females. For various reasons I had never experienced that with my mother growing up and it left a deep need. I needed to feel protected by a female. I needed to feel loved and truly prized. I needed to feel the touch of someone who cared about me and was willing to nurture me. It's funny, but once I realized that these needs were not evil, my eyes were opened. I began to notice that touch is not taboo among straight women—it's common and accepted, the rule rather than the exception.

"When I was trying to meet those needs in the lesbian lifestyle, I felt compelled. I was out of control. I endured serious physical abuse, staying in terrible relationships just so I could maintain a way to meet those needs. What a wonderful feeling it is now to have those kinds of needs met through positive relationships. I have friends and family members I'm close to who help meet those needs. I'm much more in charge of my life. I don't feel the guilt and I don't have to worry for my safety."

Christopher, another individual with whom we worked, went through a similar transformation. Like Barbara, he came to realize that his needs were not wrong, but that he was trying to satisfy them in ways that were distorted and, at best, brought only fleeting relief. We thought his summary was most fitting: "I was thirsty, but in my ignorance I drank from the wrong cup." Like Barbara and Christopher, let us seek the good within ourselves, and courageously work to nourish and express it more fully.

■ CHAPTER 6 ■
EXPRESSING YOURSELF FROM THE HEART

To know what you prefer, instead of humbly saying Amen to what the world tells you you ought to prefer, is to have kept your soul alive.

—Robert Louis Stevenson

What and how much had I lost by trying to do only what was expected of me instead of what I myself had wished to do? What a waste, what a senseless waste.

—Ralph Ellison

Admitting Our Struggles

If we want to change, we must be honest about where we are now. How can we change if we won't acknowledge the truth about ourselves and our struggles with self-control?

But it's not enough just to admit our problems to ourselves—we also need to admit them to others. Why? First, when we let others know the truth about our struggles, we can begin to have their support. Second, we bring the problem out into the open, where we can more effectively do something about it. And, third, the very process of truthfully seeing our difficulties, and then sharing them with others, helps us increase our ability to change.

Here's how it works: Remember that change comes most effectively when our hearts and minds are in line with each other—when we

92

feel the desire to change as well as *think* we need to. Unfortunately, we usually can't change how we feel just by wanting to. But if we can honestly talk about our feelings and our struggles, our desires and our goals, we can see ourselves more truthfully. We can see much that is good, along with the bad we usually focus on. Seeing the good helps to increase our confidence in our ability to change. And confidence is a *feeling* that will help us to change.

To put it all into sequence:

1. We honestly recognize the things about ourselves that we want or need to change. We also recognize the good things about ourselves.

2. We honestly share those things with others.

3. In the sharing, we more fully "own" the feelings we have, positive and negative.

4. As we do this, we find new support from others. They see our self-control problem but still see us as good persons, individuals worthy of love and respect. They also support us in our efforts to do differently.

5. This helps to increase our self-acceptance—as others accept us, "warts and all," we see ourselves more as persons of worth.

6. This will help to increase our self-confidence—we'll see ourselves as people who really can change.

7. With greater self-confidence, which is an inner feeling of worth and ability, we are able to proceed more successfully with the process of change.

In this chapter we will explain how and why this all works—and hopefully you will get started on your way to greater honesty and self-expression.

The High Cost of Faking It

This chapter is about being ourselves. Sure, that sounds simple enough, but there is great risk involved. Perhaps because of that risk, many of us fail to project on the outside the person we are on the inside. What do we do instead? Often we pretend.

Think about yourself for a moment. What do you do with the parts of yourself that you rate negatively? Is there some aspect of yourself that you find distasteful? An "unattractive and unappealing" part of your body? Some part of your personality? Shameful past behavior? Do you let others see these things? Or do you hide them?

Because of what we view as the worst parts of ourselves, we fear that others will devalue us. We begin to view ourselves negatively. In time we might actually learn to keep ourselves a secret even from ourselves. Novelist James Baldwin suggested that "the trouble with a secret life is that it is very frequently a secret from the person who lives it."[1]

Many of us spend significant time and energy on secrets and facades. What's worse, we are afraid to do that which is consistent with our positive nature as children of divine parents. How many opportunities to bless our lives and the lives of others have we missed because we feared that the world would judge us? After all, we don't want to be viewed as too religious—or perhaps foolish.

> Dean: Tim and Doug were good friends—almost more like brothers than friends. Tim loved the gospel and wanted many times to share his testimony with Doug. Doug was from a Baptist family but did not embrace any religion. Tim felt uncomfortable sharing his spiritual side with Doug. "It will ruin our friendship," he thought. "He'll think that I'm weird." With all of his heart he knew that he should share the gospel with Doug. There were many opportunities. Often Tim would feel a strong impression in his heart that Doug needed to hear his beliefs—but each time his head would overrule.
>
> One day Tim spontaneously asked Doug if he could talk to him about spiritual things. Surprisingly, Doug responded very positively. In fact, he indicated that he had been very curious about some of Tim's religious beliefs.
>
> I recently had the privilege of attending Doug's baptism; Tim performed the ordinance. In my brief conversation with Doug, he indicated how important it had been for him to hear

the gospel message. He was indeed glad that Tim had risked himself and shared his testimony with him.

Many times the fear of sharing our positive selves is just that—only a fear. But it is a real fear. Whether the news is good (like Tim's experience) or painful, finding others we can be safe with can make a lot of difference. This idea is expressed beautifully by George Eliot:

"Oh, the comfort, the inexpressible comfort of feeling safe with a person, having neither to weigh thoughts nor measure words, but to pour them all out, just as they are, chaff and grain together, knowing that a faithful hand will take and sift them, keep what is worth keeping, and then, with the breath of kindness, blow the rest away."[2]

We tend to fear self-expression particularly when we are struggling with self-control. We find ways to mask our behavior, mask our thoughts, mask our feelings. How easy it is to forget that expressions of our positive selves are incredibly healthy as we seek to develop a complementary relationship between our heads and our hearts.

Many of us become good at masking our feelings until it is too late. "How I wish I had told Mom I loved her," says one. Or, "I wonder if my good friend really knew how much I cared?" Learning to let the good desires of our hearts reach to those around us helps us and them.

In our counseling, we've seen this use of facades and hiding over and over again. In the statements that follow, some clients describe the concealment and deception involved in presenting a facade that hides their problem of self-control:

"It's like my whole life was a lie to cover up my addiction. It determined the way I related to everybody."

"I always sensed that my next achievement was the one that would bring me respect and a sense of adequacy. I kept hoping I wouldn't be ashamed and embarrassed."

"If you had asked my bishop or fellow ward members, they would have said I was an excellent Church member. I had callings of responsibility in the ward, yet I felt like I was going to hell. I don't think other people had any idea what I was struggling with, or that I even had a struggle. Those of us who deal with this kind of problem become very good at hiding it. It's a pretty lonely struggle."

"I was lacking integrity. By that I mean I really was a person split— my desires were inconsistent with some of my behaviors. Here I was married and having a good sexual relationship with my wife, but I was also sometimes alone and masturbating."

"When I sat in church I was uncomfortable because of my lifestyle, and when I was involved in the lifestyle I was uncomfortable because I really believed in the gospel."

"It was really a split-personality type thing that developed. I could work and function in church and do everything in one personality, and then if I had a chance to indulge in my addiction, I would just shift into a totally different personality."

Most of the above quotations come from those who have significant struggles. How much better it would have been if they could have shared their struggles earlier, in a safe environment, before their challenges grew so large.

Oftentimes such struggles in people's lives represent negative or distorted means of responding to legitimate emotional needs. Our need for the four A's—acknowledgment, attention, affirmation, and affection—is sometimes misdirected. Learning to express these needs and have others respond helps us to develop positive relationships. Someone once said that one great purpose of the gospel of Jesus Christ is to help us develop human and God-like relationships. Perhaps learning to express the righteous desires of our hearts increases our healthiness and prevents us from the trap of faking.

A wonderful expression by Parley P. Pratt demonstrates how the Holy Spirit can help us express ourselves from the heart.

> The gift of the Holy Spirit adapts itself to all . . . organs or attributes. It quickens all the intellectual faculties, increases, enlarges, expands and purifies all the natural passions and affections; and adapts them, by the gift of wisdom, to their lawful use. It inspires, develops, cultivates and matures all the fine-toned sympathies, joys, tastes, kindred feelings and affections of our nature. It inspires virtue, kindness, goodness, tenderness, gentleness and charity. It

develops beauty of person, form and features. It tends to health, vigor, animation and social feeling. It develops and invigorates all the faculties of the physical and intellectual man. It strengthens, invigorates, and gives tone to the nerves. In short, it is, as it were, marrow to the bone, joy to the heart, light to the eyes, music to the ears, and life to the whole being.[3]

When we hide ourselves from others, we engage in a kind of deception. But we must overcome this tendency to pretend. And we can only do so by practicing honest and open—and sometimes painful—communication with others.

Why Aren't We More Open?

In order to become more honest in our self-expression, it is crucial that we first understand why we have come to rely on deception in the first place.

In the January 1991 issue of *BYU Today* is an excerpt of Elouise Bell's book, *Only When I Laugh*. The article is entitled, "When Nice Ain't So Nice," and in it Bell decries the common tendency to turn our attention from uncomfortable truths—to be "nice" at the cost of honesty and integrity. If there were less pressure to be so nice, she suggests, perhaps we would be more real with each other, instead of putting up well-polished fronts and hiding our faults.

Noting a number of cases of child-molestation and abuse by men who are outwardly very "nice," she wonders: "If these men had been under less pressure to be 'nice,' would they have been more in touch with their dark sides—the dark side we all have—and thus more able to deal directly with violent impulses before they became actions?"[4]

Bell then explores the false self we sometimes project, quoting John Bradshaw: "You pretend a lot. You gauge your behavior by how it looks—by the image you believe you are making. You wear a mask, play a rigid role, and hide your emotions. You say you're fine when you feel hurt or sad. You say you're not angry when you are."[5]

Whether it means projecting falsehoods about ourselves or ignoring greater societal or historical truths, "Nice," Bell concludes in the end, "ain't so nice."

Bell's call for less pretending and more genuineness and integrity strikes us as sane thinking. But many of us value safe pretense over risky integrity. In a culture where we are encouraged to always put our best foot forward, maybe that's not so surprising.

It seems that we often value appearance over substance. If we valued substance, we would take the substance as it is rather than insisting it be presented in just the right light.

The Truth, Even When It's Ugly, Will Set You Free

Harry Stack Sullivan, a pioneer in the field of psychology and a champion of the importance of interpersonal relationships, underscored the significance of interpersonal honesty and integrity. He defined the cure offered by psychiatric therapy as the "expanding of the self to such final effect that the patient as known to himself is much the same person as the patient behaving to others."[6] When we are truly known to others, they see our weaknesses and our strengths, our mistakes as well as our merits.

Throughout decades of practice, Irvin Yalom, perhaps the foremost expert in group psychotherapy, has interviewed patients who have completed therapy about the single most important incident in their treatment. The most common type of incidents patients reported involved self-expression, the patients expressing their true selves—the good and the bad—to other members of the group.[7]

The patients attributed the impact of such experiences to, among other things, the fact that their fears about the effect of such expressions were not realized. "The feared catastrophe did not occur; no one left or died, the roof did not collapse."[8]

Of course, this discussion is not meant as a recommendation that we completely loose the reins of our self-expression. It is just as easy—perhaps easier—to err in the direction of destructive indulgence of negative expression. In our expressions, we must also maintain consideration for others; honesty is a poor excuse for careless or inconsiderate actions or words.

We also would not recommend continually dwelling upon anger, hostility, or resentment in order to "get it all out." While this kind of "openness" was preached for years by some psychotherapists, recent research has found that this tactic just doesn't work. In fact, such expression often serves to perpetuate rather than curtail those negative feelings. However, we must also watch that we don't err in the other direction: needlessly stifling seemingly unacceptable parts of ourselves until we cannot feel that we're loved for who we are, because no one knows the real person inside.

The Courageous Act of Being Yourself

We pay a high price for having so many censors and filters through which the thoughts of our hearts must travel before they are communicated. By being so selective in our self-expression we continually give ourselves the message, *You're not acceptable as you are.* When we are willing to express ourselves more freely, on the other hand, we give ourselves a vote of confidence.

One simple way we can practice being ourselves is to give ourselves the freedom to express our unique preferences and tastes, as opposed to being intimidated into conformity by the power of public opinion. The psychologist Abraham Maslow maintained that many of us have become separated from ourselves to the point that we fail to express our true selves even in minor matters of personal preferences and taste. Sadly enough, we often take a reading from the social barometer before we speak or act, rather than reacting honestly and from the heart.

Maslow recommends a simple procedure for freeing ourselves from social pressure when it comes to matters of preference and taste: Close your eyes if possible and "make a hush." Now you are ready to look within yourself and try to shut out the noise of the world so that you can look to the "Supreme Court" inside yourself. Then, and only then, come out and say, "I like it" or "I don't like it."[9]

The Quest for Self-Acceptance Begins with Self-Expression

The relationship between self-acceptance and self-expression is cyclical. The more we accept ourselves, the more able we are to express our true selves—no facades, no gimmicks, no editing. The more we express ourselves, the more likely we are to see that others can accept our true selves as well. Yes, we will find that there are some who will not accept us. But we also see that, in spite of their rejection, the world does not end! We remain intact, our entire selves, both good and bad. The experience of being accepted (or of being rejected without dire consequences) creates expanded feelings of self-acceptance and confidence. And this helps us in our efforts to change.

As we explore the relationship between self-acceptance and self-expression, we must understand that only one part of the equation, self-expression, is completely under our control. Let us explain: Feelings of self-acceptance are just that—feelings. As such, they are ephemeral. Everyone has had the experience of feeling great self-confidence at one moment and extreme self-reproach at another—perhaps even within the same twenty-four hours. No matter how hard we try to talk ourselves out of our feelings (to pull ourselves up by the bootstraps, so to speak) or to force other feelings upon ourselves, our success is inconsistent at best.

Self-expression, on the other hand, is a behavior. We can choose to open our mouth and make an honest, perhaps risky, statement, or we can leave it closed.

Consider the example of Sister Bronson. She was fearful as a child and never understood why. Particularly in new situations, she seemed almost paralyzed. A mission was particularly challenging for her. Each day she would make promises to herself—she would not be afraid today. She practiced her door approach, anticipating possible reactions. She practiced not being awkward.

After what seemed like an eternity, armed with various techniques and strategies, she reluctantly indicated to her companion that she would take the lead. Resisting all of her fears, she approached the next door. When she was greeted by a middle-aged man, she felt overwhelmed with fear and anxiety. Her companion quickly intervened, and they had a wonderful discussion.

Sister Bronson felt like a failure—crippled with fear. She vaguely remembered a blessing admonishing her to be herself and to express the feelings of her heart. Despite her attempts to overcome, somehow fear continued to prevail.

Interestingly, while her attempts to remove fear from her life met with continued failure, her participation in missionary work did not cease. She felt the fear and did it anyway! Although she was uncomfortable for a large portion of her first months out, she discovered that as she continued to express herself to others in her missionary labors, she gradually became more and more comfortable with the work.

Looking back, Sister Bronson realized that if she had waited until she felt the confidence, she may never have opened up. Actions are easier to control than feelings.

Conscious, effortful entry into the upward spiral of self-confidence can begin with self-expression. If you want to gain self-confidence, try expressing yourself more openly, even if it's scary. Like Sister Bronson, you may be surprised by how quickly you begin "feeling" the part you've started to play.

Self-Expression: It May Be Safer Than We Think

Mark: The case of Rachel, whom I treated for depression, provides an example of how increased self-acceptance and self-expression contribute to the process of personal growth.

For years Rachel had suffered from feelings of inadequacy and fatigue. She felt like she was working all the time but that her performance was never quite good enough. In spite of obvious successes in relationships and in her work, she still felt a nagging undercurrent of worthlessness. "It's like auto-pilot," she said. "Any time I'm not exerting conscious effort to be positive, I slip back into self-criticism." She found fault with herself when little, everyday problems arose, and significant setbacks seemed to heap up additional evidence that she was, in essence, a failure.

She envied her friends who seemed to be able to relax and enjoy life. Ironically, she observed, they were able to just let things happen because, in their lives, good things did "just happen." She saw her life as very different:

"Nothing has ever come easily for me. I've struggled for everything I've accomplished. I feel like I have to keep fighting for everything. I wish it didn't have to be that way. I wish something good would just happen, something I could enjoy without having to fight tooth and nail for it."

As Rachel explored her own style, she reflected on how harshly her parents had judged themselves, too. Of her mother, she said:

"I can see where I get it. My mom lists every day the things that she has to do, and she does them. And if she doesn't get any part of it done, she feels terrible. If she loses something, she gets irate with herself. Even if it's something small, she gets really worked up about it."

She also described her father and the messages she received from him:

"Looking back, I understand that my dad and I are both perfectionists. We're very driven and we blame ourselves a lot. He had a very bad relationship with his own father, who was very abusive; he was actually known in the community for abusing his sons. Their only use, in his eyes, was as extra work hands. My father really brought that into his relationship with me, even though the circumstances were totally different. We don't live on a farm and I'm a girl, but he still managed to give me the sense that I was never working hard enough."

Early in my counseling with her, Rachel described herself in a very critical tone as "lazy" and "passive." This self-assessment was similar to feedback she had long been receiving from her parents, especially her father. "I dreaded my dad coming home.

I still get a sinking feeling when I see him because I feel like 'I'm going to get it now!' And I did get in trouble. Usually I'd be reading or playing and he would get angry about that. 'What are you doing? Come outside and help me. Why are you sitting there reading when you could be doing something constructive?'"

Old habits die hard, but as we explored her perceptions and the feedback from her father, it became clear that she had begun to interpret her childhood experiences differently.

"As I've started looking back on it lately, I don't really see myself as lazy anymore—or at least I don't think of laziness as such a bad thing! I was *seven!* A seven-year-old girl, and he expected me, I guess, to be out plowing fields. 'Laziness.' That word has such negative connotations. If I were to hear someone described as 'very bookish, someone who likes to read and stay inside,' I wouldn't think, 'Oh, what a loser.' I would think, 'Oh, it sounds like she enjoys life.' But that's not the message I got when I was growing up. I got the message I was being bad. I should have been doing chores for my mom. Or I should have been outside helping my dad.

"I guess I learned to treat myself like my parents treated themselves and treated me. I thought I was lazy, which meant I couldn't trust myself and had to be whipped into shape. So I've been treating myself like a 'beast of burden,' thinking that's what I had to do to get anything done. And I had to get a lot done to be a worthwhile person.

"I can see why I feel the pressure to achieve. My parents yelled at me so often that I built a persona around that 'lazy' core. I tried so hard to whittle away that 'lazy' part of my personality that I actually thought it didn't exist anymore. For years I've been acting the part of a hard worker who is driven to succeed. The problem was, I could do a million things in a day and yet still think of myself as a passive, lazy person."

For years, there was a part of herself Rachel felt she could not risk expressing. Therefore, she had done everything she could to avoid laziness and passivity. Ironically, she found herself yearning for the things she was trying to deny: she longed to be the recipient of good fortune that didn't require her usual Herculean effort.

However, by the time I worked with her, she had begun to question the harshness of her self-perception. As Rachel explored the "lazy" side of herself again, she discovered that that "discarded self" contained attributes that weren't so disgusting or evil after all! In fact, expressing that side of herself brought results that were just what she had been yearning for.

She began reading for pleasure again and rediscovered a long-lost pastime that brought enjoyment and rejuvenation. She began viewing her feelings as a guide rather than a hindrance; if she was exhausted from a day's work, she took the cue and rewarded herself with rest and relaxation.

"Before, even if I was really tired and didn't have the energy to run all the way to the other side of town, I'd force myself to do it anyway because that's what was next on my list. Now if I just don't feel like doing it, I don't do it. I've eased up on myself. If I don't get something done today, I can do it tomorrow or Thursday—it's not a big deal. I think I actually get more accomplished that way because I'm more efficient. And it makes my day more enjoyable."

For Rachel, one particular unexpected benefit of her newfound self-acceptance was the most exciting of all: once free of some of the pressure she put on herself to achieve, her relationships improved.

"Rigidly adhering to my detailed little agenda every day was very solitary. I couldn't really pursue all those different objectives when I was talking to someone else, so I avoided people. It was pretty much 'me, me, me, me, me.' I could go through an entire day without seeing anyone I knew."

When she was no longer so concerned with checking off the details on her list of things to do, she found she had more energy to invest in relationships and more time to spend with people. When Rachel began trusting her feelings and expressing herself from the heart, instead of the feared metamorphosis into an unproductive slob, she actually became more productive, more satisfied with her achievements, and more content with her life in general.

The Power of Honesty and Openness

Some of the most compelling reports we've heard about the power of honesty and openness have come from LDS men and women who have struggled with feelings of homosexual attraction. In our research, we interviewed a number of such individuals.[10] Nearly every one of them talked about the great importance of sharing their struggle with others. But it wasn't easy. Participants in our research described telling others as a great risk, a risk that was extremely difficult to take.

• "Eventually I gathered my courage and showed my face at LDS Social Services to participate in my first group therapy meeting. It was hard to get myself there. I was sick all day, I was so worried, but I felt it was something I had to do."

• "The first time I went into the psychologist's office, I wouldn't even bring up the topic. Finally he started asking questions. When he came around to the topic of homosexuality I told him, 'That's what I'm struggling with.' That was the first I'd ever told anyone. It was hard because I was sure it labeled me as a totally bad person."

• "I was very reluctant to go to LDS Social Services and participate in group therapy. I'd never met another man who I knew was dealing with the problem, and I had always been afraid that I'd meet someone else with homosexual feelings and be attracted to him."

Working on issues of homosexuality will always involve some social risk, however, and participants in our research had to reach a point where it seemed worth it to take that risk.

• "To me, the problem itself was much more stressful than therapy. Having these terrible feelings and seeing no means of escape. Not dealing with it put a cloud over things. Treatment was clearly a great alternative to what the past had been."

• "As I went into therapy I had fears about my identity becoming known. I was paranoid about sitting in a lobby and having someone walk in and say, 'I know why *you're* here.' But as I began to accept the good things about myself, I began to realize that if somebody else found out it wouldn't be the end of the world."

The fears of some participants were, at least in part, realized. Some people did react negatively when told.

• "My wife felt a tremendous sense of betrayal when I told her. Even though I've never been unfaithful to her, she wondered how I could have been in her life so long while keeping something so important from her. Even now she views homosexuality as a repugnant subject. She doesn't want to talk about it, even though that means we can't communicate about all the discoveries and progress I'm making."

• "My relationship with my extended family is cordial, but it is not nearly as close as it was before they knew. On one hand, I feel a sense of rage because their reaction seems unjust. But on the other hand, I'm trying to see it from their perspective—it must have been an incredible shock."

In spite of the risks and difficulties, disclosing one's struggle brought numerous positive results as well. Those we interviewed were usually surprised to learn that others would still accept and love them, even after learning that they were dealing with feelings of homosexual attraction. Then they were more able to feel loved for their true selves, rather than for the facade they had tried to present. Paradoxically, that helped to give them added courage and strength to change.

• "It was really a positive experience to tell my friend because I finally saw that people—your friends at least—can see you for who you are, can know about it, and still not look down on you because of it."

• "I told my wife—my fiancée at the time. It was hard for her to hear. Eventually she asked, 'Well, what does it mean for us?' And I said,

'It doesn't change anything. I intend to marry you and be faithful my whole life.' In the end she said, 'I can't believe you have gone through this for years and felt like you were alone. You won't ever have to go through this alone again. Now this is our problem and we will get through it together.' That made all the difference in the world to me."

• "The bishop told me that what I had done was wrong, and he made it clear what I had to do to repent. Then he went on to the importance of self-worth and the love he had to give me."

Acceptance of others may even force a change in one's self-perception. When the disclosure of the "deep, dark secret" of homosexuality didn't lead to the feared rejection, the people we interviewed were able to stop looking at themselves as abnormal or weird. This, again, was a helpful step in their efforts to change.

• "I was surprised by the attitude my therapist had toward it. I was totally embarrassed to talk about it, but he was direct in speaking about it, and seemed to know that I really needed to get it out into the open. One of the biggest surprises was that he seemed to feel that the way I had dealt with it was natural and normal and right. That was a real blessing for me."

• "I guess I used to identify all these issues—like being intimidated in sports situations, wanting the companionship of other males—I used to identify them exclusively with homosexuality, and now I don't. Now I think they're just part of being a person on this planet. Now I view myself as a normal person having normal reactions."

Two participants even noticed a direct connection between the disclosure of their struggle to others and a decrease in the intensity of their sexual urges.

• "I can't believe how much it has helped me to open up to my friends. It's not nearly as much of a problem as it was before. I don't think about it as much."

• "When I talk about it, the desire diminishes—it's just not as strong. Instead of a secret I keep hidden, something I'm embarrassed about and never dare bring up, I've learned to be open about it—and that has made it less of a problem."

Once struggles have been shared with others, there is no longer a need to "pretend" or "live a double life" around those people. One participant described opening up to others—dropping his facade—as the event that finally allowed integration of previously separate parts of himself.

• "The first time I went to the support group, they had us introduce ourselves. When it came time for me to actually speak, I had a strange experience. I know this will sound a little crazy, but I had almost an out-of-body experience as I started talking. I had taken the book *You Don't Have to Be Gay*[11] and put the cover of an electronics catalog on it so that I would feel comfortable reading it in public. I said 'I'm a lot like this book. On the outside I appear to be a very straight individual. None of my family and none of my friends know, but on the inside I'm struggling with homosexuality.'

"I remember as I said those words, it seemed like I was sitting next to myself hearing another person say them. It didn't feel like the words were coming from me. That was such a vivid experience.

"I think that something really good—but hard—happened there, for I had to come together and integrate by saying it out loud to this group of men I didn't know. It was like I was really admitting something and really breaking down a wall. I had compartmentalized these feelings for so many years that they really weren't a part of my conscious identity, the part of me that would speak out. By getting them out I knew I could finally get to work on them."

A willingness to open up and seek help also created opportunities for participants to meet others who were dealing with similar issues. Participants now had firsthand evidence that they were not alone in their struggle.

• "I remember praying intensely at the beginning of treatment that I would be able to meet just one man in this process who would be on my level, someone I would be able to relate to and who would be able to guide me through all this. Well, I can truly say 'my cup runneth over,' because I met more than a dozen men who became my friends and helped me."

• "It was such a relief to hear others say, 'Oh, you felt like that too? You went through that too?' I had always assumed no one could understand what I was going through."

Not only did participants see that they were not alone, but meeting others with similar struggles also helped to counter their negative stereotypes about what individuals dealing with homosexuality are like.

• "In my first meeting with the LDS Social Services therapy group, I was really quite amazed to see that the other men there didn't have chandeliers hanging from their ears. By all outward appearances, they seemed to just be normal guys like me, so I felt pretty comfortable with them right from the start."

Even though a great deal of courage is required to share difficult and socially unacceptable issues with others, those we interviewed insisted that the benefits outweighed the costs. As a result of sharing their struggles with others, they were forced to revise some of their self-perceptions in positive ways. They saw that others could still love and accept them in spite of their challenges; they began to feel that maybe they weren't all that abnormal; they found solid evidence that they are not alone in their struggles; and they became aware of the distorted nature of popular perceptions of individuals dealing with homosexuality.

The struggles most of us face are not as difficult to deal with as unwanted feelings of homosexual attraction. Certainly the benefits of honesty and openness will come regardless of the problems we face.

Practicing Self-Expression

Usually when we have engaged in an ongoing struggle to resist problems of self-control, we have become better at inhibiting our desires than expressing them. Of course, there is a time and a place for inhibition, but we must develop positive ways to express ourselves as well.

Take advantage of small opportunities to give full expression to your emotions. Practicing in little ways will allow you to develop more trust in your positive desires so that you'll be able to follow them when it really counts. Here are some suggestions from Francesca Coltrera:

> • Build mini sensual experiences into your day. Set the alarm earlier so you can enjoy the cozy warmth of your bed; soak up the sun during lunch hour. . . .
> • Unleash your emotions. When something strikes you as funny, let yourself laugh explosively. Or cry over a sentimental TV commercial if you feel like it.
> • Dedicate some time to a cause that excites you. . . .
> • Don't rush through every meal—savor the tastes, smells, and textures of your food.
> • Pick a controversial subject and debate it tooth and nail with your spouse or a friend.
> • While you're doing chores, put on your favorite music and dance or belt out the words.
> • Pick an activity you enjoy—tennis, cooking exotic meals, or playing piano—and make it a goal to improve your skills.[12]

Those clients we've worked with who have given more expression to their positive desires—even in seemingly little ways like those listed above—are often surprised by the increased enthusiasm and zest for life they experience.

Long Forgotten Desires

We may have to dig around a bit more in order to redevelop our ability to express ourselves from the heart. This is especially true if we've become extremely good at denying our desires—whether out of fear or simply because the goals of our heart haven't seemed "productive" enough when we really *thought* about them. For those we've worked with, expressing themselves from the heart has often meant returning to a long-abandoned pastime or hobby. Here are some examples:

"I knew I had to spend more time relaxing again. I had become so wound up in school that I wasn't allowing myself any room to enjoy little things. Looking back now, I think that's how I got so deeply into my addiction—it was my one pleasure in life. In trying to find a better outlet, I went back to my childhood. I used to build and fly model air-planes. I started again. My adult toys are bigger than the ones I had as a kid, so it can get expensive. But it's given me something to do that is fun—something that's a complete escape from the pressure of life. In many ways it's similar to my addiction—I get completely into it to the point that I lose track of time; I look forward to doing it and fantasize about it when I'm doing something else that's boring or monotonous; I feel a complete release of tension afterwards. The difference is that I don't have to feel guilty when I'm done. I also don't feel like I wasted my time. I used to, because I was so concerned about being 'produc-tive' with every second of my time. But now I see tension release and relaxation as just as important as the other, more tangible accomplish-ments of my day."

"When I was younger I loved to cook and sew. Those were my favorite hobbies. But I got out of the habit when I started working full time. I stopped cooking and we ate out more. I stopped sewing and began buying all my clothes. I no longer worked in the yard because it was 'more efficient' to hire someone and spend my time going to meet-ings or talking on the phone. Looking back now I realize that some of those 'inefficient' activities added spice to my life. I started paying $70 a week for therapy at the same time I was paying the neighbor kid $20 a week to work in the yard. That's when it hit me—working in the yard had been my therapy! I let the kid go and I'm feeling much better now. I bought a new sewing machine and I have a little sewing corner in the bedroom. I also love to barbecue, taking my time preparing dinner while I enjoy the sights and sounds of our backyard. Now that I've picked up some of those old pastimes again, stress doesn't affect me as much."

"At first I thought it was silly when my therapist told me to dig into my closet of memories and rummage through some of my old ways of expressing myself to see if any of them still fit. But it really worked for me. My parents used to get all us kids in the car and say, 'We're going for a drive.' After reminiscing for a while about how much fun that used to be, it hit me that it had been years since I'd gone for a drive just for the sake of going for a drive. As an adult I had used my car only to get someplace else, never to enjoy the process. Now I've introduced my family to the fine art of 'going for a ride.' They love it. It's fun to be spontaneous for a change, to just drive away from the house not knowing where we'll end up. 'Right or left at this corner, kids?' Sometimes we look at houses. Sometimes we end up in the mountains. Sometimes we end up at a drive-in restaurant getting ice cream."

"I used to love music. When we were kids, my friends and I used to go down to the basement, set up a stage, and create makeshift microphones, guitars, and keyboards. We'd put two or three little AM radios on the same station, turn them all the way up, and 'jam' to the music. I bought all kinds of records and tapes. Now those records are sitting in a box in the attic. When my therapist asked me about it, I realized I hardly ever listened to music anymore. All of my presets in the car were set on talk-radio stations. Even when I did listen to music, I didn't let myself really get into it. Then my therapist gave me an assignment to start singing in the shower and in the car. I thought, 'You've got to be kidding!' But I decided to try. I found you can't do it halfheartedly, so I've really been getting into it. I came out of the bathroom the other day and my daughter had been holding a tape recorder to the door. After I tried to wrestle the recorder from her to destroy any evidence, we both just rolled with laughter. That is the most spontaneous interaction we've had for a long time, and in more ways than one I owe it to singing in the bathroom."

Though it might require a little digging, there are probably a few habits of the heart from your past as well. Perhaps you might rummage through your closet of memories and try a few on again. Once you shake off the dust, you may be surprised to discover that one or two still fit!

CHAPTER 7

DISCIPLINING YOUR HEART

If, indeed, you use the word [self-denial] in the sense of some weak sour moralists, and much weaker divines, you'll have just reason to laugh at it. But if you take it as understood by philosophers and men of sense, you will presently see her charms and fly to her embraces . . . ; for self-denial is never a duty, or a reasonable action, [but] a natural means of procuring more pleasure than you can taste without it.

—BENJAMIN FRANKLIN

The Heart's Need for Discipline

Upon learning some of the ideas expressed in this book, one woman came to a therapy session visibly upset. "You make it sound like self-control should be effortless. Well, I know that life is just not like that. After 30 years of watching my husband try to quit smoking, I just can't believe that kicking that kind of habit can be pulled off as smoothly as you make it sound. This life wasn't meant to be that easy."

She's right, of course. True self-control requires *disciplined self-expression.* If we wish to follow Christ, we cannot use our natural feelings and inclinations—what we feel like doing—as a continual and surefire guide for living our lives. There are certainly times when we, like he, must be willing to say "not as I will, but as thou wilt." (Matt. 26:39.)

So far in this book we have purposefully focused more heavily on self-expression than upon discipline. We've done this not because we feel discipline is unimportant—indeed, it is indispensable—but because we believe most people are already well familiar with the virtues of self-discipline, even to the point of self-denial. But few have a true under-standing of the importance of recognizing, developing, and expressing the desires of the heart.

It's surely true that self-control is not an easy thing. Old habits die hard. Satan does not give up his hold over us without a fight. Change and self-improvement can be difficult to attain.

But many people believe that "success is 1 percent inspiration and 99 percent perspiration." This may be true in some endeavors, but it is patently untrue with achieving lasting change in deep-seated feelings or behaviors.

We don't want people to stop "perspiring," or putting forth their best efforts. But we do believe there are ways "the best effort" can be expended more efficiently—toward setting the sail rather than rowing the boat. Our point is not that willpower is unnecessary, but simply that it is not enough. In matters of self-control, all the perspiration in the world can go to waste if there is no inspiration directing it.

Of course, while it is inadequate when used *alone*, discipline is a necessary element of self-control. If we wish to nourish the good in our hearts, we must also exert control over the evil.

Channeling our passions means denying ourselves at times, not simply for the sake of self-denial but as part of a judicious mix that includes positive and constructive self-expression.

Discipline without Disrespect

When we see our desires as only good, we engage in their unin-hibited, unprincipled, uncontrolled expression. We have referred to such expression as self-indulgence. It can be illustrated graphically as follows:

Self-Indulgence

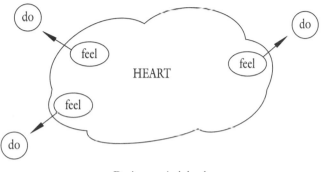

Desires are indulged

The dangers of self-indulgence were discussed earlier. Put simply, the heart makes a better servant than a master.

On the other hand, when we rule our desires with an iron hand, we engage in self-denial:

Self-Denial

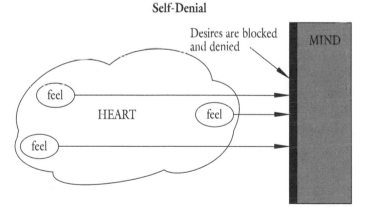

The heart makes a better servant than a master, but if we treat the heart as a riotous slave, oh what potential we destroy! When it is nourished and disciplined lovingly, the heart can be a powerfully helpful servant.

We make all kinds of efforts to educate our minds. We take classes, we learn gospel doctrine, we reason together. But how often do we attempt, as Charles W. Penrose recommended, to "school [our] feelings"?[1] Instead of "schooling" them, we often tend to engage in self-recrimination for even experiencing them. The heart can be a powerfully helpful servant, but only if we treat it with respect.

Elder Orson F. Whitney, a member of the Council of the Twelve Apostles in the first part of this century, recommended a "conquest" of our hearts. He further noted, however, that rather than obliterate our desires, such a victory should consist of the "purifying and ennobling of the passions."[2]

In the words of Dr. Allen Bergin:

[Self-control] is the ability to modulate, to rule feeling, passion, habit, and inclination, not with an iron hand, but rather with a sense of timing and regulation which maximizes outcomes for oneself and others. It is the ability to submerge oneself in feeling when it is useful, appropriate, or right, thus to enrich one's existence. It is thus the ability to delay gratification, but not to avoid it entirely. Like the steam regulator, it permits expression, but only in useful or safe channels.[3]

True self-control, then, must transcend both self-denial and self-indulgence. Certainly we must avoid doing what we feel like doing at times. However, instead of trying to cast our desires away, we must strive to recognize their value. They may be diamonds in the rough, perhaps, but diamonds nonetheless.

Respecting our desires, even as we discipline them, will allow us to inhibit them at times, but out of wisdom instead of fear. We may express them at times, but out of choice instead of compulsion. Then, rather than engaging in self-indulgence or self-denial, we may express our desires in a way that is spontaneous but within our control, in a way that is free but responsible, and in a way that is acceptable to both our minds and our hearts. In short, we will be engaging in self-control:

Self-Control

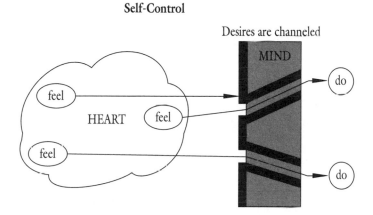

Remember the value of this kind of disciplined self-expression: When our desires are channeled instead of stifled, they remain a vital force that can be used in our lives; our energy is expressed, and we retain its power to motivate.

The Value of Inhibition

As we are working to gain self-control, some desires of the heart must be inhibited. In the "Self-Control" illustration, some of the desires of the heart were blocked rather than channeled or expressed. While we are not strong enough to resist every desire of our hearts— nor should we ever seek to do so—there is tremendous value in resisting temptation to think or feel or act in ways we know to be clearly wrong. Recall the analogy we drew between willpower and a guardrail on a dangerous stretch of highway. While we don't want to continually depend on a guardrail to keep us on the road, there may be times when it saves us from disaster. Similarly, at times willpower is all that stands between us and sin.

Religious psychotherapist Joe Dallas recognizes the importance of resistance and inhibition in the early stages of change. His conceptualization of the beginning stages of self-control, which we have altered slightly for this discussion, is outlined as follows[4]:

117

1. The destructive or undesirable behavior ceases.

2. Needs that have been satisfied through that behavior are heightened and identified.

3. Those needs begin to be satisfied in more positive, constructive ways.

The role of resistance in change, as summarized in these three steps above, deserves a more thorough exploration. We will begin with a story.

Mark: Just before my mission to Korea, in the midst of all my busy preparations, I had a couple of dreaded events I had to put on my schedule. I had bone fragments in the joint of my big toe that required an operation, and I had to have my wisdom teeth pulled. "Why not kill two birds with one stone—or at least in one day?" I reasoned, and I scheduled myself for a full day of "body work."

After surviving a morning of digging and scraping on my toe, I was put under for a session with the oral surgeon in the afternoon. After all the physical trauma I had endured (survived?), I was amazed that I felt as good as I did when friends came by to visit that evening. "Where do you hurt most?" one asked.

I had to consider before I responded: "Neither one really bothers me, I guess. In fact, I feel fine all over." Silently commending myself on my high tolerance for pain, I enjoyed the evening with friends and family. The following morning, however, I was "fine all over" no longer. My entire head rung and my foot throbbed. Soon after Mom administered the next dose of narcotic, I realized that the pain tolerance had not been my own but the relieving effect of medication.

When the pain medication was in effect, I hadn't detected the damage to my body even when I tried to tune into it. But once the mollifying effect of the medication wore off, it became crystal clear which parts of my body had taken a beating and were in need of healing.

We all know how effective medication is at deadening pain—and blinding us to our physical problems. A similar phenomenon occurs when we're entangled in problems of self-control. Specifically, although self-indulgence doesn't meet the underlying need, it provides temporary placation. In the process, we become temporarily blinded—pacified, if you will. The energy that emanates from a legitimate need is thus released in a nonlegitimate way—but it has been released nonetheless. Therefore, it no longer remains the pressing issue it once was. This can be illustrated graphically as follows:

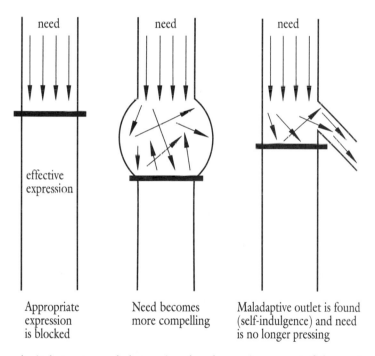

| Appropriate expression is blocked | Need becomes more compelling | Maladaptive outlet is found (self-indulgence) and need is no longer pressing |

A vital step toward change involves becoming aware of the underlying need. And a key to being able to come to that awareness is to stop the undesirable behavior. This requires inhibition and resistance—willpower. As you resist your desires, the need will grow. Hopefully, then, the appropriate channel can be unblocked, and more effective means of expression can be found:

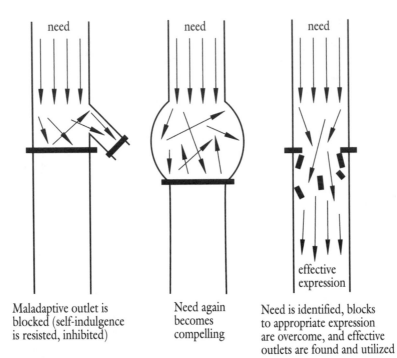

| Maladaptive outlet is blocked (self-indulgence is resisted, inhibited) | Need again becomes compelling | Need is identified, blocks to appropriate expression are overcome, and effective outlets are found and utilized |

When feelings of neediness and temptation arise in our lives, we must not simply grit our teeth and suffer through the process of resistance and self-control. Rather, it is crucial that we begin to explore the desires of our hearts, asking questions that will help us identify appropriate pathways for meeting our needs. We presented these questions earlier:

What am I feeling right now?

What do I want right now?

What happened just now? How did it contribute to the feelings I'm experiencing?

What would feel good right now?

Is there a way I can meet the needs I'm feeling that is not sinful?

Could there be benign—even healthy—desires of my heart that are adding force to this temptation?

Self-Denial for a Higher Purpose

To be effective, self-denial must primarily be used as a transitional tool. Current temptations are resisted in an effort to uncover the needs behind those temptations. Once the needs are uncovered, we must learn to meet them in ways that accord with our goals of righteousness. Of course, we will never eradicate temptation from our lives. But we can (and must) learn to make inhibition and resistance part of a multifaceted approach to coping. With this understanding, inhibition or self-denial is not seen as an ultimate show of willpower or personal victory over sin. Rather, it is the judicious choosing of which desires to express in action and which not to express, in accordance with gospel truths.

As Allen Bergin points out, self-control includes

> the ability to delay gratification, to resist the temptation of immediate rewards or pleasures in favor of more distant and often higher satisfactions, in accordance with abstract principles of right and wrong. This includes the ability to tolerate tension, discomfort, and frustration. . . .
>
> [A colleague] has said that "character is the ability to inhibit instinctive impulses in accordance with a regulative principle." That is, there is a time and place for expressiveness, but it must be regulated in terms of internal guides such as goals and ideals. Convictions imply a concept of something beyond self, beyond individual need which regulates the processes of goal direction, achievement, and management of a positive life-style. Convictions differentiate those who will behave in the "natural" way from those who aspire to the higher planes of civilization and righteousness.[5]

Dr. Larry Crabb, another religious counselor, notes that while self-discipline and self-control may appear the same on the surface, at the core they are very different.

> Let's say there are two men walking through an airport, and there's a magazine rack with pornographic magazines in the gift shop. Both men are Christians, and they both feel an urge to go look at the magazines.
>
> One man doesn't go into that shop because he is exercising self-discipline; the other doesn't go in because he is exercising self-

control. You won't be able to observe the difference because in both cases they'll walk by the rack and not expose themselves to temptation.

The difference will be evident only by exploring their motives at the moment. The person who is exercising self-discipline will internally experience it as, *This is something I should not do. Therefore, I will not do it.* The person with self-control will say all that, but then he'll go a step further. He'll say, *I really don't want to do this even though there is a part of me that does. But the deepest part of me that understands where real life is found does not want to do this, and therefore I'm honoring who I really am in Christ by walking away from it.* The difference between "want to" and "should" is a profound one.[6]

Finding the Higher Purpose:
Getting the "Feel" of What You "Know"

Acting as we know we should may not be easy, and we often must find motivation in a higher purpose. But how do we find that higher purpose, keep it in our *minds,* and eventually implant it in our *hearts?* Here's one way:

Act first, feel later.

We cannot expect to always feel like doing good—especially at first.

Feelings simply cannot be forced. For example, we cannot make ourselves feel courageous. However, we can go about acting in ways that will build our courage. Similarly, we cannot always begin with a pure desire for righteousness, but we can obey God's commandments—and that will help build our desire for good. Elder Joseph B. Wirthlin puts it quite simply: "Only in accepting our Savior and doing his will do we acquire the 'feeling to do right.' If we break the commandments, we get a 'feeling' for that too."[7]

Emphasizing that breaking the commandments of God can result from a failure of either desire *or* action, Elder Wirthlin further states: "Fundamental to most wrong-doing is a lack of desire, the absence of a strong motive or the right influence, and a deficiency in living the precepts."[8]

Our desires are not simply "there" to be accepted or rejected as they are. We can build and shape those desires through our actions. Indeed, by our actions we are building and shaping our desires every day, whether through disciplined effort toward good or through lazy indulgence along the path of least resistance.

Redefining Success

Resistance is necessary as a transitional tool and, to a limited extent, must be used throughout our lives. But, as we've emphasized before, exclusive reliance on resistance and inhibition is not the most effective method for coping with temptation on a long-term basis. Ultimately, we must work to develop to the point where we have God's law written in our hearts and "delight to do [his] will." (Psalm 40:8.)

Here's an actual example of how this can work, taken from a series of therapy sessions conducted by Mark:

> John came to therapy complaining of symptoms of depression. As I talked to him, it soon became clear that he was nurturing an anger that had built up in him over the years, anger at his feelings of being treated unfairly by others. With relish, he recounted incident after incident where he had been mistreated. While others had apparently been cruel, John had played the martyr. He had exerted unceasing, Herculean effort toward maintaining his composure in the face of abuse. In fact, John was so much "in control" of his feelings of resentment, he maintained that anger was not his problem. He wanted help with his depression, "becoming more motivated," and controlling his urges for pornography and masturbation.
>
> The following discussion occurred during one session while we were exploring John's view of "successful self-control."
>
> "If only I could control my sexual urges like I do my anger, then I'd be happy."

123

Interested, I asked, "Tell me about a time when you have been successful."

"Last week there was one day when I was real happy with how well I did. All afternoon while I was studying I was bombarded by sexual urges. I'd think about it, but I never acted on it. I never left my studying; I never masturbated. The temptation continued that night, but I never succumbed. It was hard work, but by evening I felt great. I really felt in control of my life."

Then he added, "The next day was terrible. I broke down and gave in to the temptation. All that hard work down the tube."

"The day you were able to resist the temptation to masturbate, was that success a lot like your resistance of anger?" I asked.

"Oh, yeah. I may have an incredible rush of energy, but I'm able to keep it inside. Last week I was playing pool with my roommate and I was messing up every shot. I got so mad I felt like breaking the pool stick against the wall. I felt like I could have snapped it in two with my bare hands. But I kept myself under control."

Strangely enough, when it comes to problems of self-control many of us, like John, have identified the verge of failure as success. He felt he was successful because he controlled his temper, even though he felt the heat of anger rising in him. He felt he was successful because he resisted the temptation to masturbate, even though it bombarded him all day and into the night.

As time went on, however, success came in ways John had not expected. As he explored and developed additional ways of expressing his feelings in words and actions, he was surprised to find that he spent less and less of his energy resisting. As time went on, he discovered that he was no longer spending entire days trying to beat back the relentless attack of temptation.

After about a month of therapy, John came to one session with a grin that covered his face. "I'm on cloud nine. I met a girl I used to be friends with in high school. I took her to lunch to catch up on what she's been doing and we really had a blast. We had another date Friday night and we talked for what seemed like an eternity. I don't feel like I have to hide anything from her; she accepts me as I am."

We explored this rewarding new relationship for a time. "How are you doing with the temptation to masturbate?" I finally asked, breaking his reverie.

"It hasn't really been an issue this week," John responded. "What a success!"

"It's not so much that I was successful in dealing with the temptation. It's just that I wasn't really tempted."

"What a success!" I repeated, and John smiled as he began to see my point. "What other times have there been over the past few weeks where it hasn't really been an issue?"

As John thought back, he listed several periods where masturbation just wasn't an issue, where he experienced no temptation at all. "Two weeks ago I spent the weekend involved in helping run the Special Olympics meet. Then last week my little brother was visiting from California for three days. That was a lot of fun and we stayed pretty busy. I wanted to make it fun for him and that took up all my time."

From that point on, John began to redefine successful self-control. He now saw success as avoiding times of extreme temptation as much as possible by meeting his needs in more appropriate ways. Rather than trying to restrain the full force of his anger after it had grown and swelled within him, he tried to stand up for himself immediately when he felt he was treated unfairly. Rather than spending the day trying to resist sexual temptation, he filled his schedule with more activities he found both enjoyable and fulfilling.

Barely avoiding drowning is not considered successful swimming. Avoiding divorce, in spite of years spent entertaining it as an option, does not constitute a "good marriage." Similarly, when it comes to self-control, success does not consist of full-fledged resistance at the verge of failure. Rather than intense discipline in times of crisis, the discipline in successful self-control is exerted throughout the entire process of planning our lives and then living them in ways that are agreeable and fulfilling.

We hope you can see from this discussion that success with self-control problems is not simply blocking the temptation, even in crisis, nor is it simply "letting go." Instead, true success requires an understanding of why we want and feel what we do and then finding righteous ways to satisfy those desires.

▪ CHAPTER 8 ▪
REHABILITATING YOUR HEART

We tend to think of the results of repentance as simply cleansing us from sin. But that is an incomplete view of the matter. A person who sins is like a tree that bends easily in the wind. On a windy and rainy day, the tree bends so deeply against the ground that the leaves become soiled with mud, like sin. If we focus only on cleaning the leaves, the weakness in the tree that allowed it to bend and soil its leaves may remain. Similarly, a person who is merely sorry to be soiled by sin will sin again in the next high wind. The susceptibility to repetition continues until the tree has been strengthened.

—DALLIN H. OAKS

A Mighty Change of Heart

In the last few chapters of this book we have been talking about reclaiming the power and wisdom of the heart. Yet in order to be truly reclaimed, some desires of your heart must be transformed, not simply embraced or even disciplined. In the scriptures, some of the most powerful examples of repentance and change are described as "changes of heart." When people's hearts are changed, there remains in them no more "disposition" (Mosiah 5:2) or "desire" (Alma 19:33) to do evil. Above and beyond this removal of the desire for evil, a change of heart includes a corresponding replacement with a passion for good.

The "mighty change [of heart]" (Alma 5:14) is given as a gift from God through the power of the atonement of Jesus Christ. It comes when we finally and truly yield our hearts to the workings of the Spirit.

127

(The process is described, in brief, in Mosiah 3:19.) Thus it is that the people in King Benjamin's time could exclaim that "the Spirit of the Lord Omnipotent . . . has wrought a mighty change in us, or in our hearts." (Mosiah 5:2.)

This mighty change is ultimately what will transform us from natural and fallen creatures to those who are godly in all our feelings, thoughts, and deeds.

If it's true, then, that the ultimate change must come through Christ—and it is—what can we do?

It would be displeasing to God if we were just to wait passively for him to work this marvelous miracle in us. In fact, those who wait without diligent action on their own part will never receive the blessing. We must do all we can, all that is in our power, to refine our feelings and turn our hearts to God. If we do, he will help us along the way and gradually change us, in a mighty way, from the kind of being who is "an enemy to God" to one who is a "saint" in the purest and truest sense of the word. (Mosiah 3:19.)

In *Death Comes for the Archbishop,* Willa Cather describes a change in the people of Albuquerque and Ácoma when Father Vaillant was given charge of their parish. "The holy-days, which had been occasions of revelry . . . were now days of austere devotion. The . . . Mexican population soon found as much diversion in being devout as they had once found in being scandalous."[1]

Sigmund Freud's theory allowed for this kind of change in people's lives. He attributed such changes to "displacement" and "sublimation." In other words, he suggested that raw energy—which originated as sexual or aggressive energy—could be turned to more benign, socially acceptable purposes. The underlying assumption was that the positive expression was actually a distorted or displaced expression of the original energy. Freud's theorizing has had immeasurable influence on subsequent thinking and on our society's implicit assumptions regarding the motives for human behavior.

It's probably clear that our thinking is quite different from Freud's. Rather than believing our positive, constructive behavior to be driven by base desires that have been twisted for good, we conclude that it's actually the other way around. In other words, negative, unacceptable behaviors (problems of self-control) are actually counterfeit outlets of inherently good desires.

Good Desires Gone Bad

Our passions have tremendous potential for good. However, given the inherent strength of these drives and the fact that we come to this life without experience in managing such power, they bring with them a risk and a potential for harm as well.

We believe that problems of self-control are essentially "good desires gone bad." Consider Karen, for example, who was addicted to prescription medication. She had a great desire to become more involved in intimate relationships and to achieve success in her life. However, as her attempts to do so failed, she turned to drugs in an attempt to placate feelings of loneliness and worthlessness. This diversion of positive energy toward a negative behavior in Karen's life can be presented graphically, as follows:

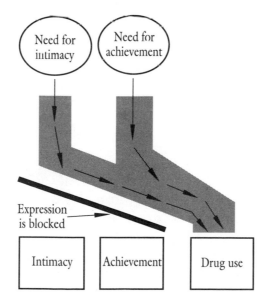

Karen approached her problem with all the willpower she could muster. To her initial relief, she found that her problem of self-control could be blocked simply by denying herself access to medication. However, such an approach left her without a more acceptable and appropriate means of expressing her desires and meeting her needs. As a result, her sense of neediness went completely unmet, continually increasing in her and thus causing future abuse to become more and more difficult to resist. This may be illustrated as follows:

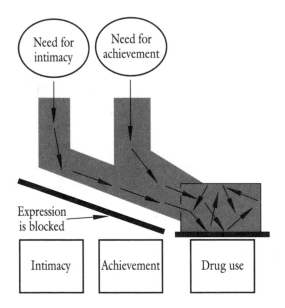

Rehabilitation of the Heart

Our approach to solving problems of self-control relies on the belief that desires, even inappropriate or unacceptable ones, can be rehabilitated. They need not simply be resisted, completely repressed, or even removed.

We believe that the process of overcoming most problems of self-control consists of two essential steps. First, the true, positive desires of our hearts—for which the unacceptable thinking or behavior has become a counterfeit—must be discovered (or often rediscovered). Second, desires are redirected to the appropriate channel of expression.

Step 1: Discover the true desires of your heart. When we are immersed in problems of self-control, we come to recognize *them* as the true desires of our hearts. While this perception is inaccurate, since the desires of the heart have been distorted and misdirected, these problems do not strike us as "alien" or "unnatural." Often we desire— we truly feel like engaging in—behaviors that at the same time we believe to be irrational, unhealthy, inappropriate, or wrong.

Remember that one reason it is so difficult to free ourselves from problems of self-control is that our true, positive desires are not readily apparent to us. Karen believed she was addicted to medication because it gave her true relief, not because she had unmet needs for intimacy and achievement.

Only when she recognized the true desires of her heart—not for drugs but for these more constructive goals—could she focus her energy on step two.

Step 2: Redirect your desires to an appropriate channel of expression. Karen gradually came to realize that she no longer expressed herself in many of the positive ways she had before her drug abuse. A few years earlier she had been through a bitter divorce, and she had since avoided intimate relationships with others as an attempt to protect herself from further hurt. She also stopped doing many of the things that once had brought her enjoyment and a sense of accomplishment, such as artwork and creative writing.

As Karen evaluated her life, she began to recognize that drugs were her way of achieving a relatively immediate relief to pain. This way of attempting to meet her needs, while quick and seemingly effective from a short-term perspective, cost her a great deal as well—it stole from her the opportunity to develop long-term means of achieving satisfaction.

Once she recognized the truth about drugs—that they were placating needs that previously had been met through emotionally intimate relationships and through art and creative writing—Karen refocused her energy. She stopped simply trying to resist drugs and started to develop those other aspects of her life. The result: as she rediscovered those other means of coping, Karen became less and less compelled by the temptation to abuse drugs.

Of course, she wasn't able to find direct expression for all her needs. But the driving force behind these unexpressed needs and her general sense of anxiety was not nearly as great as it had previously been. It was then much less difficult to redirect her energy toward an outlet preferable to drugs.

Karen's problems were not all solved by a return to her old coping skills. She discovered that she had to develop new ones as well. For instance, she began to use physical exercise and other outlets as means of coping. More importantly, she began to rely on the Lord as she had never done before. She became more devoted to him and came to rely more on his love and the peace only he could bring to her heart.

Karen's solution can be illustrated as follows:

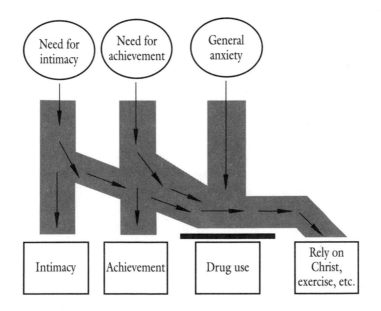

Principles of Change

The case of Karen illustrates a number of important principles we need to keep in mind as we seek changes in our lives:

Problems of self-control are often misguided attempts to meet legitimate needs.

The powerful, driving nature of legitimate needs helps account for the compelling, often addictive nature of problems of self-control.

We can learn to meet these powerful, legitimate needs in ways we find preferable to our problem of self-control.

Once we find preferable alternatives for meeting our needs, we no longer find our problem of self-control as overwhelmingly compelling. Our hearts are beginning to be rehabilitated.

As we find preferable alternatives for meeting our needs, we become more in control of our lives, more free to direct the energy of our hearts.

We can build additional positive avenues for expressing and expanding the desires of our hearts.

As our problems of self-control cease to be the sole means of expressing our hearts' desires, we eventually leave them behind, much like a snake sloughs off its old skin.

The Case of Alicia

As we have presented the principles of change, we have tried to be as complete and as forthright as we can. Unfortunately, the journey toward overcoming problems of self-control is almost never straight-forward, nor is it simple. As our clients keep reminding us, the process is often complex and always difficult.

To provide a more complete picture of the process of change, we will now provide a week-by-week account of therapy with a woman we'll call Alicia. As you read her story, see if you can observe in action the things we've talked about in this book.

SESSION ONE: Alicia, a 37–year-old woman, came to therapy

desperately anxious to gain control of her eating habits. Her problem was long-standing: she'd been called "fatso" all the way back in elementary school. By the time she was in junior high her mother had placed her on a strict diet, and she'd been able to lose most of the excess weight. Her self-esteem jumped, she became popular with her peers, and she had a lot of dates throughout high school.

In spite of her ability to maintain a "normal weight" during much of her teenage and early adulthood years, Alicia admitted that, even then, her eating habits were not ideal. One year she "starved" herself so that she'd look good in a bathing suit at a spring party. She also recounted incidents of coming home from school "depressed and lonely"—and eating food to make herself feel better. "That still goes on today," she admitted. "Sometimes I use food as a painkiller."

Alicia had four children. She reported that "with each child, I put on a little more weight. And with each child, it became increasingly difficult to lose it afterward." Her husband was supportive; her weight didn't seem to be an issue between them. "But I can tell he'd prefer me to be thinner. Now and then he does say something nice about how I used to look—and of course I take it as an insult about how I look now. He doesn't want to make love as often anymore either, whereas I have had a greater desire over the past few years."

Although she had long been concerned about her eating habits and her weight, the "last straw" for Alicia was developing diabetes. Her physician had said, "You'd better lose weight or else!" With the help of a nutritionist, Alicia had developed a diet much like the one she had followed as a teenager. In contrast to her teenage years, however, the latest attempt to control her eating was frustrating and unsuccessful:

"I know what I have to do; I'm just having a very difficult time controlling myself. At first it was just a matter of resenting that I couldn't eat what I wanted like other people can. I'd let down for a meal or two, telling myself I deserved it. But now it has become a daily problem. When I finally get the kids off to school in the morning, I tell myself I've earned a little indulgence. Then at night, with all the kids to bathe and put to bed, sometimes eating in front of the tube is the only reward I get.

"But it's been blown way out of proportion. I find myself sneaking food so that no one will know. I feel like an alcoholic at times. Then I get mad and think, 'I don't have to be ashamed of this! I'm not a terrible person. I don't beat my kids. I'm faithful to my husband. My eating is not a sin. It's really a fairly minor problem.' Then I remember what the doctor said and I realize I have to get it under control."

At the end of the first session, we asked Alicia to monitor her eating habits over the following week. We also asked her to pay careful attention to how events and her emotional reactions to those events affected her eating. "There will be some times when you do better than others," we said, "even if it's just a little better than usual. Pay attention to what happens at those times so that you can tell us about them next week."

SESSION TWO: Alicia came in for therapy discouraged. The week had not gone well. "On a scale of one to ten," we asked, "how would you rate your week?"

"Terrible," she answered.

"Give it a number. One?" we wondered.

"No, I've been more depressed than that before," she laughed. "Two or three."

"So if it's about two or three on the average, there may have been times that were as low as one and a half."

"Oh, yeah. Wednesday I was so frustrated with my five year old I was about to scream!"

"But you chose not to?"

"No, he's just a kid. I didn't scream. I just bit my tongue and sent him to his room. He had broken all the crayons in half and strewn the art supplies all over the living room. I had a homemaking committee meeting that night and I was still cleaning it up when they all got there. Wednesday was definitely a one and a half."

After exploring that night in more detail, including her emotions and her eating, we moved on. "If that night was a one and a half, and the entire week averaged two or three, there must have been some times that brought up the average. Tell us about a time that was a three and a half or a four."

"Friday night, definitely. It was the first time my husband Ned and I had been out in over a month. He's been trying to finish a major project at work, and he finally turned it in. He came home early Friday afternoon and was there to play with the kids after school. That was nice because it gave me a chance to relax. We went out Friday night to celebrate his finished project. I guess that was higher than a four. I was on cloud *nine* that night."

"What was so good about that night?"

"The main difference was that Ned was there for me. He works such long hours that sometimes I feel like I'm raising four kids on my own. But also, my sister babysat for us and when we got home the kids were all asleep and the house was clean—what a treat! To top it all off we made love that night. I really felt complete. And then I slept so peacefully, not my usual tossing and turning."

We then asked Alicia if there seemed to be a tie-in between her emotions and her eating.

"I guess so. Thursday was probably the worst. I felt like I needed some relief, and I got it through food. I hadn't connected it to the disaster Wednesday night, but I guess there's a relationship. I had noticed that when we went out Friday night I had no desire to stray from my program. I ordered a salad and was completely satisfied. I had a little of Ned's dessert and that was plenty for me. I didn't feel compelled to eat."

SESSIONS THREE THROUGH FIVE: Alicia became more and more aware of the variety of needs in her life. She began to see that she was trying to meet many of them through eating. But food, it seemed, only "filled the emotional holes" partially. She was still "hungry" emotionally. At one point she said, "I could keep eating forever and not fill those needs with food."

SESSION SIX: At the beginning of the session, we asked Alicia,

"Were there some small ways you succeeded in meeting your emotional needs this week?"

"I asked Ned to come home from work at five o'clock Thursday night. We had to get ready for a scouting banquet for my oldest boy. I knew if I tried to do it alone I'd go crazy. To my surprise he said, 'no problem.' I had assumed he would get angry and say something about needing to be at work to support the family. He's done that a few times in the past, and I had learned to not even ask. In fact, I usually just assume he won't help me when I need it, keep my mouth shut—and then resent it like the devil all the while."

"What do you think made the difference? Why did he respond differently this time?" we asked.

"For one thing, rather than keep things to myself, I asked for his help. That probably wouldn't have worked in the past, but he knows I've been under a lot of stress lately. We had a family meeting before I started therapy and everyone agreed that if I was going to do what I needed to do, I would need lots of support. I thought we were talking primarily to the kids, that Ned would remain just as involved at work, but apparently he's taken it to heart, too."

"That's great—you expressed what you needed and he responded!"

"Yeah," Alicia laughed. "I think another reason Ned has been more responsive lately is that we really made it a matter of prayer this time. In the past when I told him he spent too much time at work he would get defensive and accuse me of nagging him. But when he heard me praying for help, I think he took it much more seriously. Just putting it in a religious context helped him see it as something important.

"But I felt like I was at the end of my rope. My very life is in danger and yet I couldn't handle this eating problem on my own. That really scared and humbled me. I have always been very independent, but my eyes were opened to my need for the Lord. So I started praying for help—which was a little hard, because I have always felt selfish praying for myself. I relied on Ned too. I asked him to give me a blessing, which I rarely do. My reliance on both the Lord and on Ned has made a difference."

SESSIONS SEVEN THROUGH NINE: In the weeks that followed, we explored Alicia's independence, her tendency to meet her needs on her own rather than ask for help. Her strength and autonomy had always been a strong point and had served her well in many ways throughout her life. However, by always trying to meet her needs on her own she had denied herself many of the resources available from others.

As we tried to understand where she had developed her independent attitude, Alicia began to explore strong feelings from her childhood. She was sixth in a family of seven children. Her parents were very busy both in and out of the home. She recalled many times wanting to "cry on someone's shoulder, but everyone seemed too busy to care about the petty feelings of a little five-year-old." Instead of going to others when she was upset, Alicia would shut the door to her room and "bury my face in a pillow and sob."

She recounted an incident that occurred in the third grade. "I got in some kind of trouble in school. My dad had to come pick me up and take me home. I'm sure he was mad about whatever I did, but I remember he gave me the feeling that it was even worse that I had interrupted his work."

It became very clear that Alicia had developed the pattern of trying to keep her needs to herself, meet them on her own, and not "bother" others. Eating had always been one way for her to placate her own emotional needs. It may not have been as fulfilling as deeper relationships with others would have been. But she perceived that reaching out to others was "imposing on them," which she didn't want to do; she found this "independent" means of meeting her needs preferable. As she came to understand some of the reasons behind her eating problem, she determined that she needed to "reach out" and rely more on others rather than depending solely upon herself and upon food.

During weeks seven through nine of therapy, her ongoing

homework assignment was to pay attention to how she was already "reaching out" to others, even in small ways.

SESSION TEN: Alicia was enthusiastic when she came to the session. "I discovered that it's not really that much of an effort to reach out! It's not at all what I expected—instead of being harder, it actually takes *less* energy to be open with others. This past Wednesday it was my turn to host the homemaking committee meeting again. My house was a mess as usual, but rather than stressing out over it I just let it go. It was a risk because I was afraid of what my friends would think. But I thought, hate it or love it, I'm going to let them see the real me. I know that sounds silly—a messy house is not the 'real' me any more than a clean one is. Maybe it was more symbolic. All I know is that I felt more at ease with my friends.

"It was funny because we got into a conversation about how hard it is to keep up the facade of a woman who has it 'all together.' One of the women who always seemed flawless started opening up about some personal problems she's having. It gave us all a chance to support her. I'm not certain of it, but she may not have done that if I hadn't let down my hair a little and let her see that I have my struggles too."

Alicia's homework assignment for the week was to "keep up the good work." We suggested she keep noticing what happened as she opened up to others in small ways. We told her to keep track of what happened inside herself as well as the reactions of others.

SESSION ELEVEN: Alicia said that she tried an experiment during the week. She approached a friend to ask for advice about a frustrating problem she was having with her eight-year-old daughter. "That was new for me. I realized after we talked how unusual it was for me to be the one asking for help. Friends have always seen me as someone they can depend on—a listening ear, a shoulder to cry on, someone who's there for them in a bind. I'm very comfortable on the giving end. I'll gladly do things for others, but I don't want to be a burden so I don't usually ask when I'm the one who needs something."

We were curious. "How did you decide to take a risk like that, even with the precedent of all your habits and your history working against you?"

"I had some of those feelings of being a burden. But then I caught myself. I told myself, 'This is only an experiment. I'm taking the risk just to try it out. Teri's a good enough friend that I can count on a sincere reaction and I'll know whether I'm imposing on her.' In the end it wasn't that much of a risk."

"But a lot of people would have walked away from that risk, right?"

"Oh, yeah. In fact, *I* would have in the past."

"Your courage seems to be growing. You deserve a lot of credit for that. How did it end up?"

"She was very supportive. It was very nice. Like I said, different from what I'm used to, but nice."

Later in the session, Alicia brought up another change: "For the first time in our marriage I've begun to take the initiative in bed. Before, I would rationalize that I didn't want to be an overbearing woman. I thought I was being demure. Now I can see that I didn't want to be rejected by Ned. It would have crushed me to be turned down if he didn't want to make love when I did, so I didn't assert myself. I just waited around until he was 'in the mood' and approached me."

"What happens when you take the initiative? How does Ned react?"

"Ned loves it, of course. He teases me, 'What's come over you?' but he's grinning from ear to ear. I feel more freedom. It's just like in other areas we've talked about in my therapy. I don't feel like I have to take care of all my own needs anymore or wait around until someone decides to do something about them on their own. In fact, Ned has said he feels less and less like he has to read my mind, and he likes that."

We asked Alicia how she felt she was doing on her goal of gaining control over her eating. She responded that she was doing much better. Sometimes she still depended on food, but it was not in any way the compulsion it had once been. For the most part, she felt that her eating was now more under control--it was still difficult to manage, but it was no longer as compelling, dominating her life like it once had.

With her agreement, we determined to leave the appointment for the next session open, with Alicia calling us when she wanted to come in.

SESSION TWELVE: Three weeks later, Alicia called to set up an appointment for the following day. When she came in, she said that the previous day she had been "in crisis." Now things were fine and she wasn't sure she needed the session. We assured her that she wasn't a "burden," which gave everyone a good laugh.

She explained that she had not done well during the past week. She had been very stressed out with her kids, Ned had been gone almost all of the time, and she had relied more on food than she had for weeks. We explored her difficulties in more depth, empathizing with her problems.

Eventually we summarized: "Sounds like a rotten week. How would you rate it on a scale from one to ten?"

"Based only on the events, I'd give it a one or two. Based on how I handled it, I'd say about a three."

"Given all the difficulties, how were you able to do as well as you did?"

"I guess I just feel like I have more control now."

"When you first began therapy, you said at one point that you had experienced some times that you would rate at about one or two. Is there any difference between the ones or twos you experienced then and the ones or twos you experience now?"

"It's like night and day," she said. "I mean, in a way it's the same because so much of my life hasn't changed. But it's different because now, even when I'm down, I always know I have a way out that works better than eating. In spite of my struggles, I feel like I have moved to a new level.

"In the past I always tried to be strong. It is a positive characteristic, but I had taken it to an unhealthy extreme. I only responded when others reached out. Everyone could tell their problems to me, but I always had to be problemless. What I didn't realize was that I was leaving all these needs unmet, which I was then trying to meet through eating.

"Now I have learned to rely more on other people. I took my kids over and dropped them off at my sister's place one day last week—I just couldn't take it anymore. She was fine with that. In fact, I feel like we've become closer as I've depended on her more. I ask for and receive a lot more from Ned now, too. Even when he's busy, I feel like I can ask. If he can't, he can't; but I no longer feel like a burden simply for asking. This new attitude has improved my relationship with Ned, my relationship with Teri, and my relationship with other friends too. All of my relationships have been affected in a positive way by the changes I've made."

FOLLOW-UP: About nine months after Alicia had ended therapy, we spoke to her by phone. "It's funny," she said, "when I first came in for therapy, I was so optimistic. Maybe this would finally be the silver bullet I needed to conquer my weight problem. At that time my vision of a better future was me in a size eight bathing suit on a Caribbean beach. I had sort of a naive sense that my problems would evaporate if I lost weight, so losing weight had become my primary preoccupation.

"Well, I don't fit into a size eight bathing suit, and all of my problems are not solved. I have lost enough weight that my doctor says I'm 'out of the danger zone.' I'm walking regularly, but becoming more healthy is a gradual process. I still have 'too much' fat here and there, even though I look and feel better than before.

"But the most significant change was different from what I expected. Eating, weight, and my body are no longer my main concerns. I think that obsessing about those things was one way I was distracting myself from the real issues in my life. That has changed. I now have more invested in relationships, and I take more risks to be myself with others. I am more focused on what I think is important and I have more peace of mind."

The changes in Alicia are quite simple, in a way. As she grew up she had come to expect rejection—and had developed defense mechanisms to protect herself. Her defense included keeping her feelings to herself and being independent of others—meeting her own needs. This approach had served her well in childhood and in many respects throughout her adult life. But it failed to meet certain emotional needs, and she had come to rely on eating in an attempt to meet those needs.

Not only did she dislike her dependence on food, but it wasn't filling her needs very well either. She felt persistent neediness—an emotional hunger, if you will—in spite of her attempts to fill her needs with food.

Through discussion with us, and introspection on her own part, Alicia came to recognize what her true emotional needs were. As she experimented, she also learned that some people in her current life were much more available than she had thought. Even when they were not, she saw this as the exception rather than the rule. She also learned not to interpret any unavailability as "rejection," and she learned no longer to think of herself as a "burden."

What does Alicia's case teach us about the relation of feelings to problems of indulgence and self-control?

Before therapy, Alicia tried to limit, hide, and suppress her feelings.

She avoided expressing her anger, keeping it bottled up. She "almost screamed" at her child but "bit her tongue" instead.

She kept hurt feelings to herself. She tried to be self-sufficient as an adult, just as she had "buried her face in her pillow and sobbed" as a child.

Embarrassed, she hid her indulgent eating from others.

When she experienced sexual desire or arousal, she kept those feelings to herself, waiting for her husband to "make the first move."

Alicia felt she needed to become better at squelching her passions. But improvement actually meant she became more expressive of her heart's desires. She was able to find the true feelings of her heart and to rehabilitate them!

Here is a graphic depiction of Alicia's problem, as well as the solution:

Alicia's Problem of Self-Control

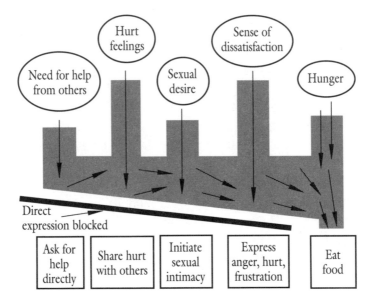

Alicia's Solution

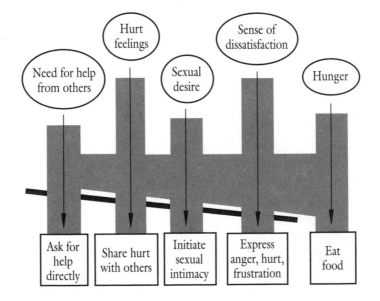

Watch Out for the Misconceptions

We have attempted, by presenting this case, to provide more detail about change. However, we find ourselves uncomfortable with several misconceptions it may foster.

First, by using therapy cases for many of our examples, we by no means wish to imply that therapy is necessary or even the most effective means of changing. Therapy is simply a laboratory of change with which we are familiar.

Second, even the case of Alicia is an oversimplified one. It does provide a more complete picture of the gradual nature of change than the other cases we have presented, but Alicia actually changed more quickly than most clients we see. Although the changes in her may appear dramatic, they occurred following years of preparation and under the influence of powerful motivating factors. Don't be discouraged if change doesn't occur that quickly for you.

Finally, we don't feel our presentation of Alicia's case (or any other we've given) demonstrates how energy-consuming the process of change can be. It is not uncommon for people to be completely "out of commission" in other areas of their lives as they grapple with these core issues and try to alter the very blueprint of their lives. This decreased capacity to cope with demands in other areas of life often makes those who are trying to change feel guilty and selfish for taking so much "time out" to work on their problem.

If this is how you feel, remember that you may have been traveling in a leaky boat for years. In order to patch the leaks, you have to stop paddling for a while. After you get underway again, however, you'll likely find that the boat travels more smoothly and requires less effort. It may even carry more people after you've repaired it! So when you find yourself troubled because you're not moving, or when other boaters glide by and ask why you're not rowing, declare without apology: "I'm fixing the boat!"

PART THREE

OVERCOMING
OBSTACLES
TO CHANGE

▪ CHAPTER 9 ▪
DEALING WITH SETBACKS

The Lord always takes people as they are, then leads gradually to what he would have them be.

—HUGH B. BROWN

Remember, You're Not the Only One

Imagine you were to attend a support group for people who struggle with problems of self-control similar to your own. At the meeting, the first person to speak describes himself as a religious person who is devoted to God but is frequently tormented by temptation and sin. He always feels guilty and sorry for sinning but finds himself losing control again and again in spite of his desires for good. Sometimes he becomes discouraged to the point where he questions his own worth—which can lead to a mire of negativity and a loss of motivation to do good. At such times, he says, it is only through the grace of God that he is able once again to see the possibility of repentance and his potential for good.

Following this introduction, another stands to speak. This man describes painful inner conflict and turmoil. He, like the first individual, wants to serve God but finds himself continually falling back into sinful habits. "Despite my best efforts, I keep doing what I don't want to do." He says it is as though there are two parts of himself that are battling it out—his inner self or his will and the temptations of his "flesh."

If you were in a meeting hearing these two reports, what would you think? Could you relate to these people? Do they sound like common people struggling with common problems? Think again! While their problems may be common, the individuals who described them certainly are not. Who are they then? Wayward souls who are hopelessly out of control? Hardened addicts who are beyond rehabilitation? Not quite. These descriptions are from great prophets of the Lord. The first was Nephi, the second Paul the apostle. Here are their words, which were the basis for the above summaries. First, consider Nephi:

"Behold, my soul delighteth in the things of the Lord; . . .

"Nevertheless, notwithstanding the great goodness of the Lord, in showing me his great and marvelous works, my heart exclaimeth: O wretched man that I am! Yea, my heart sorroweth because of my flesh; my soul grieveth because of mine iniquities.

"I am encompassed about, because of the temptations and the sins which do so easily beset me.

"And when I desire to rejoice, my heart groaneth because of my sins; nevertheless, I know in whom I have trusted.

"My God hath been my support. . . .

"O then, . . . if the Lord in his condescension unto the children of men hath visited men in so much mercy, . . . why should I yield to sin, because of my flesh? Yea, why should I give way to temptations, that the evil one have place in my heart to destroy my peace and afflict my soul? . . .

"Awake, my soul! No longer droop in sin. Rejoice, O my heart, and give place no more for the enemy of my soul.

"Do not anger again because of mine enemies. Do not slacken my strength because of mine afflictions.

"Rejoice, O my heart, and cry unto the Lord, and say: . . . O Lord, wilt thou redeem my soul? Wilt thou deliver me out of the hands of mine enemies? Wilt thou make me that I may shake at the appearance of sin?

"May the gates of hell be shut continually before me, because that my heart is broken and my spirit is contrite! . . .

"O Lord, wilt thou encircle me around in the robe of thy righteousness! O Lord, wilt thou make a way for mine escape before mine enemies! Wilt thou make my path straight before me! . . .

"O Lord, I have trusted in thee, and I will trust in thee forever. I will not put my trust in the arm of flesh; for I know that cursed is he that putteth his trust in the arm of flesh. . . .

"Yea, I know that God will give liberally to him that asketh. Yea, my God will give me, if I ask not amiss; therefore I will lift up my voice unto thee; yea, I will cry unto thee, my God, the rock of my righteousness. Behold, my voice shall forever ascend up unto thee, my rock and mine everlasting God." (2 Ne. 4:16–20, 26–35.)

Now, here is the Apostle Paul's description of his struggle:

"For we know that the law is spiritual: but I am carnal, sold under [meaning devoted to, a slave to] sin.

"For that which I do I allow not: for what I would, that do I not; but what I hate, that do I. . . .

"Now then it is no more I that do it, but sin that dwelleth in me.

"For I know that in me (that is, in my flesh,) dwelleth no good thing: for to will is present with me; but how to perform that which is good I find not.

"For the good that I would I do not: but the evil which I would not, that I do. . . .

"I find then a law, that, when I would do good, evil is present with me.

"For I delight in the law of God after the inward man:

"But I see another law in my members, warring against the law of my mind, and bringing me into captivity to the law of sin which is in my members.

"O wretched man that I am! who shall deliver me from the body of this death?

"I thank God through Jesus Christ our Lord. So then with the mind I myself serve the law of God; but with the flesh the law of sin.

"There is therefore now no condemnation to them which are in Christ Jesus, who walk not after the flesh, but after the Spirit.

"For the law of the Spirit of life in Christ Jesus hath made me free." (Rom. 7:14–25; 8:1–2.)

Did you have any inkling that the descriptions of the people in the imaginary support group were actually of prophets? Most of us are surprised because we usually exempt those people we consider to be worthy of emulation from any problems like the ones we face. Elder Marvin J. Ashton described this tendency:

> Perhaps we all live under some misconceptions when we look at each other on Sundays as we attend our meetings. Everyone is neatly dressed and greets each other with a smile. It is natural to assume that everyone else has his life under control and doesn't have to deal with dark little weaknesses and imperfections.
>
> There is a natural, probably a mortal, tendency to compare ourselves with others. Unfortunately, when we make these comparisons, we tend to compare our weakest attributes with someone else's strongest.[1]

To Elder Ashton's comments, we would add this observation by Carl Jung: "The . . . most moving dramas are not played, as we know, on the stage, but in the hearts of respectable citizens whom we pass by without a thought, and who at best show the world what battles are raging within them only if they have a nervous breakdown."[2]

The fact is, all of us struggle—none is exempt from problems of self-control. Satan would have us believe that we are alone in the problems we face, and that our struggles are undeniable evidence of our vile and worthless nature. Don't believe it! To say that these struggles are common to the human condition does not excuse or condone them. But when we accept them as common, we can begin to lift our lives up rather than continuing to beat ourselves down.

We are, truly, all in the same boat. Don't succumb to the temptation to think that you are the only one lost at sea while others are safe on the shore. We all have weaknesses sufficient to sink us—but we also have the promised assistance of our Savior. The atonement is real and its power extends to you, just as it did to Nephi and to Paul long ago, and just as it does to any others who repent and follow the Lord.

Accept Yourself in Spite of Failures and Weaknesses

In the fairy tale "Beauty and the Beast," love and acceptance transform a hideous, unfeeling creature into a being capable of selflessness, generosity, and love. What made the difference? In the animated Disney portrayal of the tale, there is a tender and touching depiction of one possible turning point. Literally "digging in" to his breakfast, the beast has made a mess. When he glances up to see Belle looking on aghast, he realizes the error of his ways. He picks up a spoon, trying to be more civilized. Clumsily, he drops the spoon from his paw.

The beast has tried to improve. He has also, to some extent at least, failed. The moment is poignant. How will Belle react? Harsh judgment? Disgust? Pretend she didn't see and hope it won't happen again? No, she picks up her cereal bowl, raises it as if to say "cheers," and slurps up her breakfast. Obviously relieved and encouraged, the beast follows suit.

What can we learn from this fairy tale?

Encouragement and acceptance are far more conducive to growth than criticism and negativity.

As we raise our children, direct our employees, or teach our students, most of us apply this great wisdom. We would never withhold affection because a baby mispronounced his first "mama." We would never spank a toddler because she fell as she began to learn to walk.

We rely on encouragement and acceptance in our work with others. Yet how many of us have learned to apply the same rule as we view ourselves, trying to improve our own behavior? Consider the words of Carl Jung:

> That I feed the hungry, that I forgive an insult, that I love my enemy in the name of Christ—all these are undoubtedly great virtues. What I do unto the least of my brethren, that I do unto

Christ. But what if I should discover that the least amongst them all, the poorest of all the beggars, the most impudent of all the offenders, the very enemy himself—that these are within me, and that I myself stand in need of the alms of my own kindness—that I myself am the enemy who must be loved—what then? As a rule, the Christian's attitude is then reversed; there is no longer any question of love or long-suffering; we say to the brother within us "Raca," and condemn and rage against ourselves. We hide it from the world; we refuse to admit ever having met this least among the lowly in ourselves. Had it been God himself who drew near to us in this despicable form, we should have denied him a thousand times before a single cock had crowed.[3]

An awareness of our weaknesses, while uncomfortable, reminds us how inadequate we are to cope with the problems we face. Only when we are willing to come face to face with the worst within ourselves will we have any hope of gaining control over it. That is because only then do we recognize our absolute need for the Savior. Ironically, as Larry Crabb points out, we ultimately succeed in gaining self-control "by allowing ourselves to be aware of the parts of our souls that we are helpless to change. We need to ask ourselves, am I in touch with things within me that are so bad, so wrong, and so weak, that no amount of self-discipline or effort can take care of them? . . .

"Being in touch with what you really cannot handle is a way to keep self-control functioning as a work of the Spirit, because then you are in touch with your dependence."[4]

Remember, Progress Occurs Gradually

Change can come quickly; a little miracle, a bit of insight, a personal revelation. However, President Ezra Taft Benson, in an effort to help us avoid discouragement, provided this reminder that spiritual growth and repentance can also be gradual:

We must be careful, as we seek to become more and more god-like, that we do not become discouraged and lose hope. Becoming Christlike is a lifetime pursuit and very often involves growth and change that is slow, almost imperceptible. The scriptures record remarkable accounts of men whose lives were changed dramatically, in an instant, as it were: Alma the Younger, Paul on the road to Damascus, Enos praying far into the night, King Lamoni. Such astonishing examples of the power to change even those steeped in sin give confidence that the Atonement can reach even those deepest in despair.

But we must be cautious as we discuss these remarkable examples. Though they are real and powerful, they are the exception more than the rule. For every Paul, for every Enos, and for every King Lamoni, there are hundreds and thousands of people who find the process of repentance much more subtle, much more imperceptible. Day by day they move closer to the Lord, little realizing they are building a godlike life. They live quiet lives of goodness, service, and commitment. They are like the Lamanites, who the Lord said "were baptized with fire and with the Holy Ghost, and they knew it not." (3 Ne. 9:20.)[5]

Along the same lines, Elder Bruce R. McConkie gave the following reassurance:

Ultimately, if I am to be saved in the kingdom of God, I have to be born again, which means I have to die as pertaining to carnal and evil things and become alive as to the things of the Spirit, the things of righteousness. If I am to inherit a celestial kingdom, I have to be sanctified, cleansed every whit from sin.

Now these things are a process. There are instances in our revelations that talk about being born again where it is as though someone were born again in an instant, as though his soul was sanctified in a moment. These occasions are so rare and so miraculous that they get written up in the scriptures themselves. But in most cases, the matter of being born again is a process. It comes by degrees. The matter of sanctifying a soul is a process. It comes step upon step and degree upon degree. We get a portion of perfection now and a greater portion later on.

We have the obligation to be as perfect as our Father in heaven is perfect. That is our ultimate objective. We don't obtain that in one leap or one step, but we go degree by degree. Maybe I am an individual who needs to pay tithing or to keep the Word of Wisdom or to perfect my moral standards or to avoid carnal and evil things of this sort or that. Maybe I am a person who needs to go to sacrament meeting or whatever. I have to determine what I have to do in my personal case in order to cleanse and perfect my soul. In order to crucify the old man of sin and become alive in Christ, I must make a personal plan of salvation, and I will perfect my soul—if I ever do—by degrees, not all at once. . . .

We just go degree by degree and step by step. Every time we manage to keep a commandment and become master of ourselves in a particular area, we grow in the things of the Spirit so that we will be able to keep a greater law and do additional things that were not previously possible. In that course and in that process, we manage to work out our salvation.

We will not be ready for glory and exaltation the moment we die. But if we chart a course and if we determine in our hearts what we are going to do and be and the reward that we are going to obtain, we will continue to pursue that course in the paradise of God, and we won't deviate from it. There will be a day when we will possess, receive, and inherit all things.[6]

Don't despair when change doesn't come overnight. As the Lord reminds us, we must grow line upon line, precept upon precept, here a little and there a little. (See 2 Ne. 28:30.) Take it one step at a time.

A Yardstick for Change

Mark: When I was younger, my mother used to measure our growth by marking a spot on the wall every year. It was fun to see the progress—to compare our height to our brothers' height at the same age, to chart our growth spurts during the teenage years. Mom's simple method gave us tangible evidence that we really were changing—growth that had been imperceptible from day to day became obvious by the end of the year.

Spiritual growth is even less obvious than physical development. Like the markings on the wall, we must find a way to remind ourselves of the progress we are making. Try keeping a record. On a scale of one to ten, rate your level of success in coping with your problem of self-control. At first you may wish to rate each hour of the day. As you improve, you can rate the success of individual days, and then, later, your success from week to week.

Keeping a record of your success in this way helps you see that you're not a "complete failure" when you give in once to temptation, just as you're not a complete success when you resist temptation for a single day. Change occurs gradually. Hopefully you will be able to see movement toward your goal, even if it doesn't happen all at once.

Another advantage of this kind of evaluation: No matter how bad things seem to get, we can look back at our records and focus on the positive, on times when things were a bit more as we want them to be. When things seem to be falling apart, ask yourself what you were doing during the successful times. How can you do more of what worked? By focusing and building on those times, we perpetuate the positive. There is positive energy in our lives, even when things seem to be hopeless. We can tap into that positive flow even if it seems to be only the tiniest brook. That approach will be much more productive than allowing ourselves to be carried along by a great river of negativity and despair.

Refuse to Be Paralyzed by Discouragement and Guilt

Guilt, sorrow, and pain are necessary, even key, elements of the repentance process. The description of Alma the Younger provides a poignant example of the power of such sorrow:

"I was racked with eternal torment, for my soul was harrowed up to the greatest degree and racked with all my sins.

"Yea, I did remember all my sins and iniquities, for which I was tormented with the pains of hell; yea, I saw that I had rebelled against my God, and that I had not kept his holy commandments.

"Yea, and I had murdered many of his children, or rather led them away unto destruction; yea, and in fine so great had been my iniquities, that the very thought of coming into the presence of my God did rack my soul with inexpressible horror.

"Oh, thought I, that I could be banished and become extinct both soul and body, that I might not be brought to stand in the presence of my God, to be judged of my deeds." (Alma 36:12–15.)

As we seek to comprehend the proper attitude toward sin and repentance, we should not allow the magnitude and depth of Alma's guilt to confuse us into thinking it continued for weeks or months. Alma went *through* the guilt and sorrow; he did not become mired in it permanently:

"And now, for three days and for three nights was I racked, even with the pains of a damned soul.

"And it came to pass that as I was thus racked with torment, while I was harrowed up by the memory of my many sins, behold, I remembered also to have heard my father prophesy unto the people concerning the coming of one Jesus Christ, a Son of God, to atone for the sins of the world.

"Now, as my mind caught hold upon this thought, I cried within my heart: O Jesus, thou Son of God, have mercy on me, who am in the gall of bitterness, and am encircled about by the everlasting chains of death.

"And now, behold, when I thought this, I could remember my pains no more; yea, I was harrowed up by the memory of my sins no more.

"And oh, what joy, and what marvelous light I did behold; yea, my soul was filled with joy as exceeding as was my pain!

"Yea, I say unto you, my son, that there could be nothing so exquisite and so bitter as were my pains. Yea, and again I say unto you, my son, that on the other hand, there can be nothing so exquisite and sweet as was my joy." (Alma 36:16–21.)

Once Alma tasted the redemptive power of Jesus Christ, he could "remember [his] pains no more" and was "harrowed up by the memory of [his] sins no more." His sorrow was a necessary step in the process, and not the end state of his repentance.

The importance of experiencing sorrow and guilt as temporary (though necessary) elements of repentance becomes apparent when we consider the effect of these emotions upon our ability to function. Recall that in the midst of his sorrow, Alma fell to the earth and became dumb, weak, and helpless. (See Mosiah 27:19; Alma 36:10.) While he was paralyzed by guilt for a time, after he had fully experienced the pain necessary for repentance he was completely freed from guilt's bonds. In fact, he was more active and motivated than ever:

"But behold, my limbs did receive their strength again, and I stood upon my feet, and did manifest unto the people that I had been born of God.

"Yea, and from that time even until now, I have labored without ceasing, that I might bring souls unto repentance; that I might bring them to taste of the exceeding joy of which I did taste; that they might also be born of God, and be filled with the Holy Ghost." (Alma 36:23–24.)

The sons of Mosiah, who had joined Alma in his sins, also were willing to let go of their guilty feelings once they had repented. Then they got to work spreading the gospel:

"And they traveled throughout all the land of Zarahemla, and among all the people who were under the reign of king Mosiah, zealously striving to repair all the injuries which they had done to the church, confessing all their sins, and publishing all the things which they had seen, and explaining the prophecies and the scriptures to all who desired to hear them.

"And thus they were instruments in the hands of God in bringing many to the knowledge of the truth, yea, to the knowledge of their Redeemer." (Mosiah 27:35–36.)

Rather than becoming paralyzed by guilt, the sons of Mosiah became energized by their experience. After receiving, with Alma, a small taste of hell when they were rebuked by the angel, they were motivated to help others:

"The sons of Mosiah . . . returned to their father, the king, and desired of him that he would grant unto them that they might . . . go up to the land of Nephi that they might preach the things which they had heard, and that they might impart the word of God to their brethren, the Lamanites—

"That perhaps they might bring them to the knowledge of the Lord their God, and convince them of the iniquity of their fathers; and that perhaps they might cure them of their hatred towards the Nephites, that they might also be brought to rejoice in the Lord their God, that they might become friendly to one another, and that there should be no more contentions in all the land which the Lord their God had given them.

"Now they were desirous that salvation should be declared to every creature, for they could not bear that any human soul should perish; yea, even the very thoughts that any soul should endure endless torment did cause them to quake and tremble.

"And thus did the Spirit of the Lord work upon them." (Mosiah 28:1–4.)

President Lorenzo Snow coined the phrase: "As man now is, God once was; as God now is, man may be."[7] Obviously, he recognized the importance of becoming perfect. But was he a perfectionist, engaging in harsh judgment and recrimination of those who do not measure up? Hardly. Rather, he reminded us that weaknesses are inherent to our mortal existence and encouraged us not to be overwhelmed with discouragement because we aren't perfect here and now.

> The Apostle Peter . . . told the Savior on a certain occasion that though all men forsook him he would not. But the Savior, foreseeing what would happen, told him that on that same night, before the cock crowed, he would deny him thrice, and he did so. He proved himself unequal for the trial; but afterwards he gained power, and his mind was disciplined to that extent that such trials could not possibly affect him. . . .
>
> If the husband can live with his wife *one day* without quarreling or without treating anyone unkindly or without grieving the Spirit of God in any way, that is well so far; he is so far perfect. Then let him try to be the same the next day. But supposing he should fail in this his next day's attempt? That is no reason why he should not succeed in doing so the third day. . . .
>
> If the Apostle Peter had become discouraged at his manifest

160

failure to maintain the position that he had taken to stand by the Savior under all circumstances, he would have lost all; whereas, by repenting and persevering he lost nothing but gained all, leaving us too to profit by his experience. The Latter-day Saints should cultivate this ambition constantly which was so clearly set forth by the apostles in former days. . . .

We must not allow ourselves to be discouraged whenever we discover our weakness. We can scarcely find an instance in all the glorious examples set us by the prophets, ancient or modern, wherein they permitted the Evil One to discourage them; but on the other hand they constantly sought to overcome, to win the prize, and thus prepare themselves for a fulness of glory.[8]

Milton W. Russon, former president of the Bountiful Utah Val Verda Stake, added this insightful warning against becoming discouraged:

Discouragement is not the Lord's method—it's Satan's. Satan emphasizes your weaknesses—the Lord, your ability to overcome. Satan urges immediate perfection to make you feel inadequate; the Lord leads you to perfection. . . . If you hear a voice that leaves you feeling weaker [and] more doubtful about your capability of overcoming sins, if it continues to remind you of past mistakes and sins that you have already repented of, then it is not the Spirit of the Lord. The Lord seeks to strengthen you, to give you the power to overcome problems. He wants you to recognize your weaknesses and then do something about them.[9]

In spite of our determination to do right, we will falter at times. Even when we do, all is not lost! Let us allow our failures to remind us of our humanity and our need for the Savior. Then let us humbly put aside our preoccupation with our own sins and tap into his power to help us change.

Build a Support System

The path to greater self-control is a difficult one. Don't try to tread it alone! As young children we were taught the value of the buddy system. As we grow older we tend to forget and try to make it on our own. Earlier we talked of giving up the illusion of self-sufficiency and learning to rely upon God. We must also learn to find reliable mortal helpers, and lean upon them when we need it.

To our knowledge, every successful rehabilitation program for addicts (it doesn't matter what the addiction is) recognizes the importance of a support system and uses it as a key in treatment. In many treatment programs, group members share phone numbers and call each other in times of temptation or stress. Great strength is gained as we share frustration and discouragement, as well as the satisfaction of success. Apparently, when it comes to gaining greater self-control, self-help only goes so far.

Steven Cramer, a Church member who struggled for years to overcome a lifelong habit of pornography (leading eventually to excommunication), identifies the unwavering support of family and friends as the key reason he didn't give up in spite of repeated failures. In his book, *The Worth of a Soul,* he tells of his son's support at a crucial time:

> About three weeks before he was to leave for his mission, my oldest son came home from BYU. By this time, I had been swept back into the enslavement of pornography for some time. I had tried to resist and failed so many times that I had totally given up. I felt that I was now ready for suicide or any escape I could find. None of my children knew about my addiction to pornography. Thus, you can imagine this sweet boy's shock as he was looking through my den for some genealogy records and discovered my hidden briefcase full of pornographic magazines.
>
> This sweet and spiritual boy who had kept himself pure and innocent for nineteen years, how crushed he must have been. And yet, he never once allowed this terrible discovery to isolate him from me. Rather, he began to pour out his love and support upon me. Refusing to accept my failures as permanent, he launched a "change Dad's attitude" campaign. All over the house he began taping 3 X 5 cards—on my mirror, on the bedroom door, in the stairway, on the refrigerator, etc. The following are some of the things he wrote:
>
> "You were sent here to succeed, and YOU WILL."
>
> "I believe in you!"
>
> "You *CAN* do it, you will do it, you *ARE* doing it!"
>
> "Dad, I love you! You are the GREATEST, and I would not

trade you for anyone or anything. You are a good man; please begin to believe it."

"You can't be too bad with a wife, two sons, six daughters, two sets of parents, brothers and sisters loving you, respecting you, praying for you, wanting you to succeed, wishing they could help you, knowing how good you are."

"You get points just for hanging on. (I thought about this one a lot and still do.) Congratulate yourself and keep it up. Endure in faith to the end."

"With so many other people convinced you are worth loving and forgiving, why can't you love and forgive yourself?"

"Forgive yourself 70 X 7. Start now. Think of the past 490 things you've done wrong and forgive yourself of them, bad as they may be. Let yourself be the good man you really are."

What a remarkably forgiving attitude he had, when he could have been so easily crushed by disappointment in me. He really made me want to try again.[10]

Once he was freed from the chains of sin and his painful excommunication was over, Steven Cramer recognized the crucial role of his support system in helping him change:

How grateful I am that of my family—my wife, my children, my parents, my brothers and sisters, my in-laws, my Bishop, and Home Teacher—not one of them ever gave up on me. . . .

I discovered God's love for his children through my family's forgiveness.

From the moment of my confession, my selfless wife was able to look beyond her own pain to the needs of saving the family. . . .

Through the years of struggle, my family's attitude was that we were all in this together. Though I never deserved their love or forgiveness, their actions always affirmed:

We still love you. We don't understand what you are going through, but it must be awful for you, and we want to help. We still need you, and we want you back as a part of us. No matter how long this takes, you can count on us to see it through with you.[11]

Others have also emphasized the vital importance of having an effective support system. Here's what some have said:

"I always thought it was best to keep these kinds of struggles to myself, and I did for years. But when I did open up to my wife, I was surprised by her support. And it came in some unexpected ways—I've struggled with depression, and when I shared some of my feelings with her she picked up a tape on depression for me. When I was really going through some difficult times and had to go on a business trip, she bought a Church music tape for me to listen to. Her support has made all the difference in the world."

"When I began attending a therapy group regularly, I learned that the group is a place where it's safe to share my struggles. The other members of the group have already experienced what I'm going through, so they are very supportive."

"I have struggled for years with feelings of homosexual attraction. The counselor I had been meeting with said I would never change and I might as well give in to it. I felt I had come to a dead end. But when I told a close friend, he talked with me, prayed with me, supported me, and encouraged me to keep trying. He convinced me I should seek counseling again and helped me get in touch with LDS Social Services. I never thought anyone would accept me when they learned about my struggles. But not only did he accept me, he became an invaluable resource."

Don't Become Complacent

Faltering once doesn't mean you've failed. Neither does successful avoidance of a problem mean you've got it made. Elder Hugh B. Brown wrote, "So far as we can see there is no goal at which we may 'arrive' and arriving, abide. Life is an infinite search leading toward an ideal which forever leads forward and forever recedes."[12]

The Lord is certainly pleased with our successes. However, his message is one of repentance—whether we are doing well or are in need of much more improvement. Interestingly, to those most in need of improvement he offers assurance that as often as they repent they will be forgiven (Moro. 6:7–8), while to those who are doing well, a warning is issued: "But this much I can tell you, that if ye do not watch yourselves, and your thoughts, and your words, and your deeds, and observe the commandments of God, and continue in the faith of what ye have heard concerning the coming of our Lord, even unto the end of your lives, ye must perish. And now, O man, remember, and perish not." (Mosiah 4:30.)

We must find a balance—on the one hand we must be "anxiously engaged" (D&C 58:27) in seeking to overcome our weaknesses, while on the other hand we must know that, ultimately, we shall succeed only through the power of Christ. As Moroni wrote: "If men come unto me I will show unto them their weakness. I give unto men weakness that they may be humble; and my grace is sufficient for all men that humble themselves before me; for if they humble themselves before me, and have faith in me, then will I make weak things become strong unto them." (Eth. 12:27.)

As we conclude, we leave this final testimony of the Lord's grace. Of all the words you have read in this book, we hope that these will reach the deepest part of your heart. The road before you will almost certainly be rocky, but the rewards can be very great. Whatever you do, do not try to traverse the path on your own. You are a child of your Father in heaven, and you are precious to him. Never think that you are not worthy of his love, or that he is unable to help you. His love for you transcends any problem with which you may struggle. If you will only open your heart to that love, it will change your life in lasting and powerful ways.

∎ NOTES ∎

Chapter 1—It Takes More Than Willpower

1. Ella Wheeler Wilcox, "Will," *Poems That Touch the Heart*, comp. A. L. Alexander (New York: Doubleday, 1986), p. 138.
2. William Ernest Henley, "Invictus," *One Hundred and One Famous Poems*, comp. Roy J. Cook (Chicago: Contemporary Books, 1958), p. 95.
3. Daniel M. Wegner, Joann W. Shortt, Anne W. Blake, and Michelle S. Page, "The Suppression of Exciting Thoughts," *Journal of Personality and Social Psychology*, March 1990, pp. 409–18.
4. Benjamin Hoff, *The Tao of Pooh* (New York: Dutton, 1982), pp. 68–69.
5. Richard G. Scott, "Finding the Way Back," *Ensign*, May 1990, p. 75.
6. Ezra Taft Benson, "Born of God," *Ensign*, Nov. 1985, p. 6.
7. Catherine Thomas, New Testament class handout, 1988.
8. Ezra Taft Benson, "A Mighty Change of Heart," *Ensign*, Oct. 1989, p. 4.
9. Eugen Herrigel, in *Zen in the Art of Archery* (New York: Vintage Books, 1989), pp. viii–ix.
10. Scott, "Finding the Way Back," pp. 74–76; emphasis added.
11. Benson, "A Mighty Change of Heart," p. 2.
12. Lewis M. Andrews, *To Thine Own Self Be True: The Relationship Between Spiritual Values and Emotional Health* (New York: Doubleday, 1987), pp. 62–63.
13. Viktor Frankl, *Man's Search for Meaning* (New York: Pocket Books, 1984), p. 17.
14. Ezra Taft Benson, *A Witness and a Warning* (Salt Lake City: Deseret Book, 1988), p. 33.

Chapter 2—The Motivating Power of the Heart

1. Abraham Maslow, "Self-actualizing and Beyond," in *The Pleasures of Psychology* (New York: New American Library, 1986), p. 299.
2. Benson, "Born of God," pp. 6–7.
3. Maslow, "Self-actualizing and Beyond," pp. 300–301.
4. Robert Epstein, "How to Get a Great Idea," *Reader's Digest*, Dec. 1992, p. 102.
5. Quoted in Michael Ray and Rochelle Myers, *Creativity in Business* (New York: Doubleday, 1986), p. 71.
6. Frankl, *Man's Search for Meaning*, pp. 60–61.
7. Ibid., pp. 94–95.

Chapter 3—The Powerful But Unruly Heart

1. Joseph B. Wirthlin, "There Am I in the Midst of Them," *Ensign*, May 1976, p. 56.
2. Seymour Epstein, "Cognitive-experiential Self Theory: Implications for Developmental Psychology," in Megan R. Gunnar and L. Alan Sroufe, eds., *Self Processes and Development*, v. 23 (Hillsdale, New Jersey: Lawrence Erlbaum Associates, 1991), p. 86.
3. Arthur Koestler, *The Act of Creation* (London: Hutchinson & Co., 1969), pp. 213–14.
4. M. Scott Peck, *The Road Less Traveled* (New York: Simon and Schuster, 1978), p. 53.
5. Mihaly Csikscentmihalyi, *Flow: The Psychology of Optimal Experience* (New York: Harper & Row, 1990), p. 18; emphasis added.
6. Ibid.
7. Nathaniel Branden, *The Psychology of Self-Esteem* (Los Angeles: Bantam Books, 1969), p. 119.
8. Much of this section was inspired by Dallin H. Oaks, *Pure in Heart* (Salt Lake City: Bookcraft, 1988).
9. David O. McKay, *Conference Report*, Oct. 1951, p. 6.
10. Dean C. Jessee, ed., *Personal Writings of Joseph Smith* (Salt Lake City: Deseret Book, 1984), pp. 263–64; spelling standardized.

Chapter 4—Tuning In to the Wisdom of Your Heart

1. Robert Ornstein, *The Psychology of Consciousness*, 2nd ed. (New York: Harcourt Brace Jovanovich, 1977), p. 12.

2. Ibid., p. 116.
3. Gordon B. Hinckley, "The Continuing Pursuit of Truth," *Ensign*, April 1986, p. 5.
4. Quoted in Walter Mischel, *Introduction to Personality*, 4th ed. (New York: Holt, Rinehart and Winston, 1986), p. 209.
5. James E. Faust, "Father, Come Home," *Ensign*, May 1993, p. 37.
6. Jeffrey R. and Patricia T. Holland, *On Earth As It Is in Heaven* (Salt Lake City: Deseret Book, 1989), p. 89.
7. Ibid., p. 37.
8. The near-death experience referred to is described in Melvin Morse, *Closer to the Light* (New York: Ivy Books, 1990), p. 141.
9. *Hymns* (Salt Lake City: The Church of Jesus Christ of Latter-day Saints, 1985), no. 241.

Chapter 5—Nourishing the Good in Your Heart

1. These terms were taken from Gilbert Ryle, *The Concept of Mind* (New York: Barnes & Noble, 1949), pp. 83–84.
2. Bruce R. McConkie, *Mormon Doctrine*, 2nd ed. (Salt Lake City: Bookcraft, 1966), p. 556.
3. Parker Pratt Robison, *Writings of Parley Parker Pratt* (Salt Lake City: Deseret News Press, 1952), pp. 52–53, 55–56.
4. Quoted in Truman G. Madsen, *Four Essays on Love* (Provo, Utah: Provo Communications Workshop, 1971), p. 36.
5. *Book of Mormon Student Manual, Religion 121–122* (Salt Lake City: The Church of Jesus Christ of Latter-day Saints, 1979), pp. 310–11.
6. Summarized from Martha Nibley Beck and John C. Beck, *Breaking the Cycle of Compulsive Behavior* (Salt Lake City: Deseret Book, 1990), p. 192.
7. Andrews, *To Thine Own Self Be True*, p. 148.
8. Beck and Beck, *Breaking the Cycle of Compulsive Behavior*, p. 261.

Chapter 6—Expressing Yourself from the Heart

1. James Baldwin, *Another Country* (New York: Dell, 1962), p. 170.
2. George Eliot, quoted in *The Treasure Chest*, ed. Charles L. Wallis (New York: Harper and Row, 1965), p. 102.
3. Parley P. Pratt, *Key to the Science of Theology*, 4th ed. (Liverpool: Albert Carrington, 1877), pp. 101–2.

4. Elouise Bell, "When Nice Ain't So Nice," *BYU Today*, Jan. 1991, p. 3.
5. Ibid., p. 4.
6. Harry Stack Sullivan, *Conceptions of Modern Psychiatry* (New York: W. W. Norton, 1940), p. 237.
7. Irvin Yalom, *The Theory and Practice of Group Therapy* (New York: Basic Books, 1985), p. 27.
8. Ibid.
9. Abraham Maslow, "Self-actualizing and Beyond," pp. 302–3.
10. The examples in this section are taken from A. D. Byrd and M. D. Chamberlain, "Dealing with Issues of Homosexuality: A Qualitative Study of Six Mormons," *Association of Mormon Counselors and Psychotherapists Journal*, 19 (1993): 47–87.
11. Jeff Konrad, *You Don't Have to Be Gay* (Newport Beach, California: Pacific Publishing House, 1987).
12. Adapted from Francesca Coltrera, "You *Can* Be More Passionate," *Redbook*, Feb. 1993, p. 110.

Chapter 7—Disciplining Your Heart

1. *Hymns*, no. 336.
2. Orson F. Whitney, *The Life of Heber C. Kimball* (Salt Lake City: Stevens & Wallis, 1945), p. 65.
3. Allen Bergin, "Toward a Theory of Human Agency," in *Suggested Readings in LDS Values and Human Behavior* (Salt Lake City: The Church of Jesus Christ of Latter-day Saints, 1980), p. 62.
4. A more detailed and specific description of Joe Dallas's model, which is used in treatment of homosexuality, can be found in *Desires in Conflict: Answering the Struggle for Sexual Identity* (Eugene, Oregon: Harvest House, 1991), chapter 6.
5. Bergin, "Toward a Theory of Human Agency," p. 61.
6. Larry Crabb, "The Sin in Self-Discipline," *Discipleship Journal*, Issue 44, p. 19.
7. Joseph B. Wirthlin, "There Am I in the Midst of Them," p. 56.
8. Ibid.

Chapter 8—Rehabilitating Your Heart

1. Willa Cather, *Death Comes for the Archbishop* (New York: Vintage Books, 1971), p. 117.

NOTES

Chapter 9—Dealing with Setbacks

1. Marvin J. Ashton, "On Being Worthy," *Ensign*, May 1989, p. 20.
2. Carl G. Jung, *Psychological Reflections: Selections*, ed. Jolande Jacobi (New York: Harper Torchbooks, 1961), p. 216.
3. Carl Jung, quoted in Victor Gollancz, *Man and God* (Boston: Houghton Mifflin, 1951), pp. 234–35.
4. Crabb, "The Sin in Self-Discipline," p. 20.
5. Benson, "A Mighty Change of Heart," p. 5.
6. Bruce R. McConkie, 1976 New Zealand Area Conference Report, p. 44.
7. Lorenzo Snow, *Deseret Evening News*, 15 June 1901, p. 1.
8. Lorenzo Snow, *Journal of Discourses* (Liverpool: William Budge, 1880), 20:190–91; emphasis added.
9. Milton W. Russon, Val Verda Stake conference address, Aug. 20, 1978.
10. Steven Cramer, *The Worth of a Soul* (Springville, Utah: Cedar Fort, 1983), pp. 80–81.
11. Ibid., p. 82, back cover of book.
12. Hugh B. Brown, *Eternal Quest* (Salt Lake City: Bookcraft, 1956), p. 15.

▪ INDEX ▪